Achieving QTS: Reflective Readers

Reflective Reader: Primary Professional Studies
Sue Kendall-Seatter
ISBN-13: 978 1 84445 033 6 ISBN-10: 1 84445 033 3

Reflective Reader: Secondary Professional Studies
Simon Hoult
ISBN-13: 978 1 84445 034 3 ISBN-10: 1 84445 034 1

Reflective Reader: Primary English
Andrew Lambirth
ISBN-13: 978 1 84445 035 0 ISBN-10: 1 84445 035 X

Reflective Reader: Primary Mathematics
Louise O'Sullivan, Andrew Harris, Margaret Sangster, Jon Wild, Gina Donaldson and
Gill Bottle
ISBN-13: 978 1 84445 036 7 ISBN-10: 1 84445 036 8

Reflective Reader: Primary Science
Judith Roden
ISBN-13: 978 1 84445 037 4 ISBN-10: 1 84445 037 6

Reflective Reader: Primary Special Educational Needs
Sue Soan
ISBN-13: 978 1 84445 038 1 ISBN-10: 1 84445 038 4

Achieving QTS

Reflective Reader
Primary Mathematics

Louise O'Sullivan, Andrew Harris, Margaret Sangster, Jon Wild, Gina Donaldson and Gill Bottle

Learning Matters

First published in 2005 by Learning Matters Ltd.

British Library Cataloguing in Publication Data
A CIP record for this book is available from the British Library.

ISBN-13: 978 1 84445 036 7
ISBN-10: 1 84445 036 8

Cover design by Topics – The Creative Partnership
Project management by Deer Park Productions
Typeset by PDQ Typesetting Ltd
Printed and bound in Great Britain by Bell & Bain Ltd, Glasgow

Learning Matters Ltd
33 Southernhay East
Exeter EX1 1NX
Tel: 01392 215560
Email: info@learningmatters.co.uk
www.learningmatters.co.uk

Contents

Introduction   1

1 The nature of mathematical understanding   7

2 Teaching children to think mathematically   17

3 Number: Learning to count and understand place value   29

4 Mental and written calculation strategies   37

5 Contexts for children's mathematical thinking   46

6 Problem-solving   56

7 Making decisions about mathematics and ICT   72

8 Effective teaching of mathematics   83

9 Catering for a range of mathematical abilities   91

References   101

Index   107

Introduction

The *Reflective Readers* series supports the *Achieving QTS* series by providing relevant and topical theory that underpins the reflective learning and practice of primary and secondary ITT trainees.

Each book includes extracts from classic and current publications and documents. These extracts are supported by analysis, pre- and post-reading activities, links to the QTS Standards, a practical implications section, links to other titles in the *Achieving QTS* series and suggestions for further reading.

Integrating theory and practice, the *Reflective Readers* series is specifically designed to encourage trainees and practising teachers to develop the skill and habit of reflecting on their own practice, engaging with relevant theory and identifying opportunities to apply theory to improve their teaching skills.

The process of educating individuals is broader than the specific areas of educational theory, research and practice. All humans are educated, socially, politically and culturally. In all but a few cases humans co-exist with other humans and are educated to do so. The position of an individual in society is determined by the nature and quality of the educational process. As a person grows up, emerging from childhood into adulthood, their social and political status is dependent on the educational process. For every task, from eating and sleeping to reading and writing, whether instinctive or learnt, the knowledge and experience gained through the process of education is critical. Humans are educated, consciously and subconsciously, from birth. Education is concerned with the development of individual autonomy, the understanding of which has been generated by educational, sociological, psychological and philosophical theories.

The position of the teacher in this context is ambivalent. In practice each teacher will have some knowledge of theory but may not have had the opportunity to engage with theories that can inform and improve their practice.

In this series, the emphasis is on theory. The authors guide the student to analyse practice within a theoretical framework provided by a range of texts. Through examining why we do what we do and how we do it the reader will be able to relate theory to practice. The series covers primary and secondary professional issues, subject areas and topics. There are also explicit links to Qualifying to Teach Standards (QTS) that will enable both trainees and teachers to improve and develop their subject knowledge.

Each book provides focused coverage of subjects and topics and each extract is accompanied by support material to help trainees and teachers to engage with the extract, draw out the implications for classroom practice and to develop as a reflective practitioner.

While the series is aimed principally at students, it will also be relevant to practitioners in the classroom and staffroom. Each book includes guidance, advice and examples on:

- the knowledge, understanding, theory and practice needed to achieve QTS status;
- how to relate knowledge, theory and practice to a course of study;
- self reflection and analysis through personal responses and reading alone;
- developing approaches to sharing views with colleagues and fellow students.

Readers will develop their skills in relating theory to practice through:

- preparatory reading;
- analysis;
- personal responses;
- practical implications and activities;
- further reading.

Primary mathematics

This book has been written as part of the Learning Matters series on achieving Qualified Teacher Status (QTS) to complement the two previous publications, *Primary mathematics: Knowledge and understanding* and *Primary mathematics: Teaching theory and practice.*

As a development of trainees' and teachers' understanding of mathematics education, this book provides extracts from journals and books on key issues surrounding primary mathematics teaching. Some of the extracts are from classic articles such as Plunkett on calculation and Skemp on instrumental and relational learning. These were milestones in thinking about how children learn mathematics and underpin how we work with children today. Other extracts are drawn from recent research or are contributions to current debates about how we teach mathematics. The work from the Netherlands leads the world in teaching children how to calculate and how mathematics is better taught in contexts. Britain itself is renowned for its work on problem-solving and investigating. Many countries are introducing SATs just at a time when we in Britain are beginning to evaluate their contribution and influence. The days when mathematics was considered a culture-free subject are long gone and there are challenges ahead to make mathematics a successful and relevant subject for all the children in our education system.

The extracts have been chosen to take you on from the skills and knowledge of teaching into territories where your beliefs and approaches are challenged. The extracts are briefly placed in context, discussed and analysed. You are asked to reflect on your own experience of mathematics and teaching the subject. Further reading is suggested to enable you to explore the topic further.

All chapters are referenced to the Standards for Qualified Teacher Status required by the Teacher Development Agency (TDA – formerly the Teacher Training Agency, TTA) in order support your development towards meeting the standards to achieve QTS.

We hope that you enjoy 'reading around' primary school mathematics education and that you gain a sense of history as well as further knowledge of the beliefs which underpin this important subject. Through the process of thought and debate with others, you will be stimulated to develop a well-informed and critical approach to the teaching of primary mathematics. This will mean reading the work provided in this book critically, examining what is said with care, enriching your own thinking with further reading and deciding how it will influence your own practice.

This book will help you to:

- engage the issues at a theoretical level with reference to key texts in primary mathematics;
- explore the teaching of mathematics in the primary stage of education;
- reflect on your own principles and development as a teacher and consider how this impacts on your work in the classroom.

Each chapter is structured around the key reflective prompts what, why and how. Each prompt is linked to a short extract. You will:

- read a short analysis of the extract;
- provide a personal response;
- consider the practical implications;

and have links to:

- supporting reading;
- the QTS Standards.

A note on extracts

Where possible, extracts are reproduced in full but of necessity many have had to be cut. References to other sources embedded within the extracts are not included in this book. Please refer to the extract source for full bibliographical information about any of these.

Authors

Louise O'Sullivan has worked in primary schools in Kent since 1992. She moved into higher education in 2000 and now works at Canterbury Christ Church University as a Principal Lecturer in Primary Mathematics. She has completed a Masters Degree in Educational studies. Her main interests are in children's written and mental calculation strategies.

Andrew Harris is a Senior Lecturer in Primary Education at Canterbury Christ Church University. After teaching in schools in Derbyshire and Gloucestershire, he moved into higher education and worked as a Senior Lecturer in Primary Mathematics Education at St Martin's College, Ambleside. He is a co-author (2005) of *Teaching Mathematics in the Primary School* (Continuum).

Gina Donaldson is a Senior Lecturer at Canterbury Christ Church University. She was a primary school teacher for eleven years and has completed a Masters Degree, which included research into children's problem-solving strategies. She is the author of *Successful Mathematics Leadership in Primary Schools* (Learning Matters, 2002).

Dr Margaret Sangster is a Senior Lecturer at Canterbury Christ Church University. She has taught across the primary school age-range and was a deputy head and a maths advisory teacher before moving into higher education. She is currently a mathematics education tutor on the primary undergraduate and postgraduate programmes. Her particular interests are children's understanding of mathematical pattern, the effective teaching of mathematics and the use of generic teaching strategies.

Jon Wild has worked in the primary education sector for 18 years, initially in London and then in southeast Kent, holding posts as deputy head teacher and head teacher. He is a Senior Lecturer within initial teacher training at Canterbury Christ Church University and is involved in the development of the Education Faculty's eLearning dimension. He was a contributor to the Canterbury Christ Church University primary mathematics team's first publication, T*eaching Mathematics in the Primary School* (Continuum, 2005).

Dr Gill Bottle has worked in primary education for over twenty years. She is particularly interested in Early Years and has written about early mathematics for several academic and practitioner journals. Gill was the coordinator for *Teaching Mathematics in the Primary School* (Continuum, 2005). In September 2005 she took up a post in the Primary Department at the University of Gloucestershire.

Series editor

Professor Sonia Blandford is Pro-Vice Chancellor (Dean of Education) at Canterbury Christ Church University, one of the largest providers of initial teacher training and professional development in the United Kingdom. Following a successful career as a teacher in primary and secondary schools, Sonia has worked in higher education for nine years. She has acted as an education consultant to ministries of education in Eastern Europe, South America and South Africa and as an adviser to the European Commission, LEAs and schools. She co-leads the Teach First initiative. The author of a range of education management texts, she has a reputation for her straightforward approach to difficult issues. Her publications include: *Middle Management in Schools* (Pearson), *Resource Management in Schools* (Pearson), *Professional Development Manual* (Pearson), *School Discipline Manual* (Pearson), *Managing Special Educational Needs in Schools* (Sage), *Managing Discipline in Schools* (Routledge), *Managing Professional Development in Schools* (Routledge), *Financial Management in Schools* (Optimus), *Remodelling Schools: Workforce Reform* (Pearson) and *Sonia Blandford's Masterclass* (Sage).

Acknowledgements

Every effort has been made to trace the copyright holders and to obtain their permission for the use of copyright material. The publisher and author will gladly receive information enabling them to rectify any error or omission in subsequent editions.

The author and publisher would like to thank the following for permission to reproduce copyright material:

Anghileri, J, 'Development of division strategies for Year 5 pupils in ten English schools', *British Educational Research Journal* vol. 27 no. 1, 2001. Reproduced with kind permission of Taylor & Francis Ltd, http://www.tandf.co.uk/journals; Barnes, C, 'Too much reading', *Mathematics Teaching* no. 190 (2005), Association of Teachers of Mathematics. Reproduced with kind permission of © Christine Barnes; Black, P and Wiliam, D, *Inside the black box: assessment for learning in the classroom* by Paul Black, Christine Harrison, Clare Lee, Bethan Marshall and Dylan Wiliam. Copyright © 2004 Dylan Wiliam. Reproduced by permission of nferNelson Publishing Company Ltd. of The Chiswick Centre, 414 Chiswick High Road, London W4 5TF UK. All rights reserved including translation. nferNelson is a division of Granada Learning Limited, part of ITV plc. This work may not be photocopied or otherwise reproduced by any means, even within the terms of a Photocopying Licence, without the written permission of the Publishers; Cooper, B, 'Assessing National Curriculum mathematics in England: exploring children's interpretations of Key Stage 2 tests in clinical interviews', *Educational Studies in Mathematics* 35 (1): 19-49 1998, Kluwer Academic Publishers 49 (1): 1023, 2002 Kluwer Academic Publishers. Reproduced with kind permission of Kluwer Academic Publishers; Cooper, B and Harris, T, 'Children's responses to contrasting "realistic" mathematics: just how realistic are children ready to be?', *Educational Studies in Mathematics* 49 (1): 1023, 2002 Kluwer Academic Publishers. Reproduced with kind permission of Kluwer Academic Publishers; Corbett J, 'School practice', *British Journal of Special Education* vol. 28 no. 2 June 2001/DfES; Reproduced with kind permission of Blackwell Publishing Ltd; Eyre, D and McClure, L, *Curriculum provision for the gifted and talented in the Primary school: English, mathematics, science and ICT*, David Fulton 2001. Reproduced with kind permission of David Fulton Publishers www.fultonpublishers.co.uk; Floyd, A (ed), *Developing Mathematical Thinking,* Addison Wesley/Open University Press, 1981; Houssart, J and Evans, H, 'Approaching algebra through sequence problems: Exploring children's strategies', *Research in Mathematics Education* 5, 2003. Reproduced with kind permission of Hilary Evans, Jenny Houssart and QCA; Hughes, M, 'Bridge that gap', *Child Education* 63 (2), 1986 Scholastic. Reproduced with kind permission of © Martin Hughes; Jones, L, *Mathematics teaching* (1994) Association of Teachers of Mathematics. Reproduced with kind permission of Lesley Jones; Kelly, P, 'Children's experiences of mathematics' in *Conference Proceedings of British Society for Research in Learning Mathematics* (BSRLM) vol. 23 no. 2. Reproduced with kind permission of Peter Kelly; McGuinness, C, *From thinking skills to thinking classrooms*, DfES 1999. Reproduced with kind permission of DfES/ Crown Copyright; Monaghan, F, 'Thinking better – Using ICT to develop collaborative thinking and talk in mathematics', *British Society for Research in Learning Mathematics*, School of Education, University of Birmingham. Reproduced with kind permission of Frank Monaghan; Montague-Smith, A, *Mathematics in nursery education*, David Fulton 1997. Reproduced with kind permission of David Fulton Publishers www.fultonpublishers.co.uk; Passey, D et al. *The motivational effect of ICT on pupils*, DfES 2004. Reproduced with kind permission of Don Passey; Perks, P, 'The interactive whiteboard: Implications for software and design', *British Society for Research in Learning Mathematics*, School of Education, University of Birmingham. Reproduced with kind permission of Pat Perks; Pratt, N, 'Mathematics as thinking', *Mathematics Teaching* no. 181 (2002) Association of Teachers of Mathematics. Reproduced with kind permission of Nick Pratt; Skemp, R, 'Relational understanding and instrumental understanding', *Mathematics Teaching* no. 77 (1977) Association of Teachers of Mathematics. Reproduced with kind permission of Valerie Skemp; Thompson, I (ed), *Issues in teaching numeracy in primary schools,* Open University Press 2004, reproduced with kind permission of the Open University Press/McGraw-Hill Publishing Company; Thompson, I (ed), *Enhancing primary mathematics teaching,* Open University Press 2004. Reproduced with kind permission of the Open University Press/McGraw-Hill Publishing Company; Thompson, I and Bramald, R, *An investigation of the relationship between young children's understanding of the concept of place value and their competence at mental addition*, funded by the Nuffield Foundation 2000-2002. University of Newcastle 2002; van den Heuvel-Panhuizen, M, *Common sense in mathematics education: proceedings of 2001.* The Netherlands and Taiwan Conference on Mathematics Education, 19-23 Nov 2001, Freudenthal Institute, Utrecht University. Reproduced with kind permission of Marja van den Heuvel-Panhuizen; Visser, J, 'Mathematics, inclusion and pupils'. *Mathematics Teaching* no. 179, Easter Conference Supplement, DfES/*Mathematics Teaching* 2002. Reproduced with kind permission of © John Visser.

1 The nature of mathematical understanding

Introduction

In this chapter mathematics in the primary school is considered from three different perspectives which are interlinked. The first is that the mathematics curriculum is politically and socially influenced and is subject to change (Brown, 1999). The second is that when considering the learning of mathematics, successful learners develop two intrinsic strands, which Skemp (1977) labelled 'instrumental' and 'relational', and that these two strands have recurred with different names throughout the subject's subsequent development. And finally, the perspective of the children is considered through research by Kelly (2003), who explores the use of mathematics in real settings. Each extract provides only a small glimpse of the nature of mathematical understanding in primary schools and, having raised your awareness of these perspectives, will provide a prompt to further exploration of the social and political influences on mathematics education as well as the nature of the subject itself.

Swings of the pendulum

Before you read this extract, you may be interested in reading the transcript from a BBC 'File on Four' programme which gives a vivid glimpse of the political scene in relation to mathematical research: *Academic freedom and evidence-based policy* (BERA website for research intelligence, 75, April 2001; **www.bera.ac.uk/ri/no75/index.html**). Professor Margaret Brown was involved in this discussion.

Extract: Brown, M (1999) 'Swings of the pendulum', in Thompson, I (ed) *Issues in teaching numeracy in primary schools*, p3. Buckingham: Open University Press.

Introduction

Ever since numeracy has been part of the curriculum for a significant proportion of the population in England, there has been a tension between accurate use of calculating procedures and the possession of the 'number sense' which underlies the ability to apply such procedures sensibly. These two positions can be broadly characterized as 'procedural' and 'conceptual', respectively.

Alongside this has been a different type of tension between individualistic 'progressive' philosophies emphasizing the importance of autonomy of both pupils and teachers in order to lead to personal development and empowerment, and 'public education' philosophies emphasizing a greater degree of state intervention in the curriculum and in teaching methods in order both to protect the equal entitlement of pupils and to meet the skilled person power requirements of the state.

Over the years the pendulum has swung back and forth in both these dimensions, depending on both social and economic contexts. In prosperous times personal autonomy and conceptual approaches have had the edge, whereas high unemployment and internationally uncompetitive industries have tended to fix the state's attention on the uniform teaching of procedural skills in Numeracy. Equally the political context has been important since it was determined whose were the most powerful voices.

As with the inescapable tensions between the fundamental notions of cultural norms and individual rationality, and of freedom and equality, which respectively underlie the two dimensions, it is probably both proper and necessary that the emphases should shift from time to time to adapt to prevailing philosophies and circumstances.

Analysis

In this extract Brown discusses the freedom to choose or follow a prescribed curriculum and teaching style. She links this with 'procedural' and 'conceptual' mathematics. One might interpret these two terms as teaching calculations and exploring relationships within mathematics. Is there a direct relationship between prescription and procedural mathematics or between conceptual mathematics and autonomy?

Brown describes a political stance where government (through the DfES and QCA in England) exercises the degree of influence on the curriculum and teachers' actions. In England, some would argue that the introduction of the National Curriculum (1989) was generally acceptable but the Standard Assessment Tasks (SATs) that followed in 1991 altered the delivery of the curriculum. The assessment of mathematics which currently exists is very different from the recommendations in the TEGAT Report (DES, 1988). SATs originally set out to measure children's success in applying their mathematics through a series of practical tasks.

Personal response

Compare the current methods of assessing mathematics in the National Tests (pencil-and-paper tests) with the TEGAT approach. What are the advantages of a task or pencil-and-paper test model in terms of administration, measuring types of knowledge and influence on the teaching of mathematics?

Brown refers to the 'requirements of the state'. Other subjects such as music and history do not appear to have this element of 'requirement'. To what extent should this be a driving factor of the mathematics curriculum? Studying only mathematics used in real life would significantly narrow the curriculum (and possibly not cater for those destined to be engineers, architects, economists and accountants). Is there justification for a broader view to be taken of mathematics as a unique discipline?

Analyse where primary school mathematics currently lies on Brown's pendulum.

Extract: Brown, M (1999) 'Swings of the pendulum', in Thompson, I (ed) *Issues in teaching numeracy in primary schools*, p14. Buckingham: Open University Press.

Postscript
The National Numeracy Strategy Framework, circulated in 1999, just over a century since the previous national curriculum was abandoned, prescribes not only an extremely detailed curriculum, year by year, for primary mathematics, but also an additional requirement specifying the type of activities which should take place in each lesson, and for how long.

While only the broader outlines are technically statutory, there are strong pressures to implement the detail since schools are inspected regularly by the Office for Standards in Education (OFSTED), which has power to advertise publicly those which are substandard, which may send them into a downward spiral leading to closure.

Analysis

Brown's view of how inspection regimes uphold the delivery of the National Numeracy Strategy and the consequences of failing to comply to perceived OFSTED expectations can determine the success or failure of a school, implies a 'conform or else' approach. Is this so, or is there room to manoeuvre? Discuss this with colleagues and teachers in different schools and analyse to what extent Brown's view is verified by how OFSTED has influenced the teaching of mathematics.

Relational understanding and instrumental understanding

Before you read the following extract, read:

- Tall, D and Thomas, M (2002) 'A tribute to Richard Skemp', in Tall, D and Thomas, M (eds) Intelligence, learning and understanding in mathematics – a tribute to Richard Skemp. Flaxton, Australia: Post Pressed, at **www.warwick.ac.uk/staff/David.Tall/downloads.html**.

Extract: Skemp, R (1977) 'Relational understanding and instrumental understanding'. *Mathematics Teaching*, 77, pp20–6.

A theoretical formulation

There is nothing so powerful for directing one's actions in a complex situation, and for co-ordinating one's own efforts with those of others, as a good theory. All good teachers build up their own stores of empirical knowledge, and have abstracted from these some general principles on which they rely for guidance. But while their knowledge remains in this form it is largely still at the intuitive level within individuals, and cannot be communicated, both for this reason and because there is no shared conceptual structure (schema) in terms of which it can be formulated. Were this possible, individual efforts could be integrated into a unified body of knowledge which would be available for use by newcomers to the profession. At present most teachers have to learn from their own mistakes. For some time my own comprehension of the difference between the two kinds of learning which lead respectively to relational and instrumental mathematics remained at the intuitive level, though I was personally convinced that the difference was one of great importance, and this view was shared by most of those with whom I discussed it. Awareness of the need for an explicit formulation was forced on me in the course of two parallel research projects; and insight came, quite suddenly, during a recent conference. Once seen it appears quite simple, and one wonders why I did not think of it before. But there are two kinds of simplicity: that of naivety; and that which, by penetrating beyond superficial differences, brings simplicity by unifying. It is the second kind which a good theory has to offer, and this is harder to achieve.

A concrete example is necessary to begin with. When I went to stay in a certain town for the first time, I quickly learnt several particular routes. I learnt to get between where I was staying and the office of the colleague with whom I was working; between where I was staying and the university refectory where I ate; between my friend's office and the refectory; and two or three others. In brief, I learnt a limited number of fixed plans by which I could get from particular starting locations to particular goal locations.

As soon as I had some free time, I began to explore the town. Now I was not wanting to get anywhere specific, but to learn my way around, and in the process to see what I might come upon that was of interest. At this stage my goal was a different one: to construct in my mind a cognitive map of the town.

These two activities are quite different. Nevertheless they are, to an outside observer, difficult to distinguish. Anyone seeing me walk from A to B would have great difficulty in knowing (without asking me) which of the two I was engaged in. But the most important thing about an activity is its goal. In one case my goal was to get to B, which is a physical location. In the other it was to enlarge or consolidate my mental map of the town, which is a state of knowledge.

A person with a set of fixed plans can find his way from a certain set of starting points to a certain set of goals. The characteristic of a plan is that it tells him what to do at each choice point: turn right out of the door, go straight on past the church, and so on. But if at any stage he makes a mistake, he will be lost; and he will stay lost if he is not able to retrace his steps and get back on the right path.

In contrast, a person with a mental map of the town has something from which he can produce, when needed, an almost infinite number of plans by which he can guide his steps from any starting point to any finishing point, provided only that both can be imagined on his mental map. And if he does take a wrong turn, he will still know where he is, and thereby be able to correct his mistake without getting lost; even perhaps to learn from it.

The analogy between the foregoing and the learning of mathematics is close. The kind of learning which leads to instrumental mathematics consists of the learning of an increasing number of fixed plans, by which pupils can find their way from particular starting points (the data) to required finishing points (the answers to the questions). The plan tells them what to do at each choice point, as in the concrete example. And as in the concrete example, *what has to be done next is determined purely by the local situation*. (When you see the post office, turn left. When you have cleared brackets, collect like terms.) There is no awareness of the overall relationship between successive stages, and the final goal. And in both cases, the learner is dependent on outside guidance for learning each new 'way to get there'.

In contrast, learning relational mathematics consists of building up a conceptual structure (schema) from which its possessor can (in principle) produce an unlimited number of plans for getting from any starting point within his schema to any finishing point. (I say 'in principle' because of course some of these paths will be much harder to construct than others.)

This kind of learning is different in several ways from instrumental learning.

1. The means become independent of particular ends to be reached thereby.

2. Building up a schema within a given area of knowledge becomes an intrinsically satisfying goal in itself.

3. The more complete a pupil's schema, the greater his feeling of confidence in his own ability to find new ways of 'getting there' without outside help.

4. But a schema is never complete. As our schemas enlarge, so our awareness of possibilities is thereby enlarged. Thus the process often becomes self-continuing, and (by virtue of 3) self-rewarding.

Taking again for a moment the role of devil's advocate, it is fair to ask whether we are indeed talking about two subjects, relational mathematics and instrumental mathematics, or just two ways of thinking about the same subject matter. Using the concrete analogy, the two processes described might be regarded as two different ways of knowing about the same town; in which case the distinction made between relational and instrumental understanding would be valid, but not that between instrumental and relational mathematics.

But what constitutes mathematics is not the subject matter, but a particular kind of knowledge about it. The subject matter of relational and instrumental mathematics may be the same: cars travelling at uniform speeds between two towns, towers whose heights are to be found, bodies falling freely under gravity, etc. etc. But the two kinds of knowledge are so different that I think that there is a strong case for regarding them as different kinds of mathematics. If this distinction is accepted, then the word 'mathematics' is for many children indeed a false friend, as they find to their cost.

Analysis

Skemp's work on instrumental and relational learning is considered to be a landmark in the history of mathematics education. Brown's reference to procedural and conceptual understanding is a current-day reference to the ideas proposed by Skemp in this article. In this extract, he attempts to explain his thinking using the analogy of knowing routes within a town. Explore the relationship between instrumental learning and learning mathematics by rote.

Personal response

To what extent is there a relationship between instrumental learning and the generation of misconceptions and errors?

One of the difficulties with problem-solving and investigation is children's limited ability to transfer knowledge to new situations (Hughes *et al.*, 2000). Does Skemp's theory go any way to explaining why this might be so? Can his theory help us to decide what kind of knowledge and learning will enable children to become better problem-solvers?

Are instrumental and relational learning mutually exclusive? To answer this, consider yourself in the role of mathematics learner. What type of understanding do you have of a specific maths topic? Now reflect on the mathematics you have seen taught or you have taught. Has the teacher set out to provide procedures/instrumental learning or relational learning? Is this affected by the topic being taught or is it the preferred way of teaching? Research at King's College London (Askew *et al.*, 1997) identified the most effective teachers as 'connectionists'. These are teachers who relate the mathematics to previous work and other areas of the mathematics curriculum. With a colleague, identify the connections you could make if you were teaching the topic of money.

Consider how Skemp's theory sits with the National Curriculum requirements for using and applying mathematics.

Exploring children's experiences of mathematics

Before you read the following extract, read:

- Nunes, T and Bryant, P (2000) 'Mathematics under different names', in *Children doing mathematics*. Oxford: Blackwell.

Extract: Kelly, P (2003) 'Children's experiences of mathematics'. *Conference Proceedings of British Society for Research In Learning Mathematics* **(BSRLM), 23(2), pp37–42.**

A semi-structured interview was used to explore primary children's conceptions of mathematics by eliciting descriptions of their experiences and understandings relating to mathematics in various in school and out of school contexts. Categories of description, representing these conceptions, were then constructed from this data. Those aspects relating to mathematics knowledge utilisation are reported here.

Conception 1: Labourer

The children have a very restricted view of use: the described mathematics is used directly in other mathematics which is exactly the same, or in tests where the tested mathematics is exactly the same. It is not seen as being useful anywhere else:

> I've used these ideas in my maths book, there are lots of questions like these. I haven't used it anywhere else, but it is useful to know so you get them all right. (Colin)

This view of use relates closely to the nature of 'what' is learned and 'how' it is learned in the conception. In working without understanding, children are easily led to make links based on superficially similar but actually unrelated features. For example, sometimes the children latch on to words to associate use with other contexts. On these occasions the only link is the actual word: its meaning and use in the two contexts are otherwise unrelated:

> I used the brackets in English. When we are writing we use brackets for something and if we didn't have enough room in the story you'd put brackets. (Denise)

Conception 2: Mechanic

Mathematics is seen as being used in exactly the same way in different contexts, be they mathematical or otherwise. Thus it is used in exams or tests where there may be a slight change in presentation, wording or context. Similarly the children identify the unproblematic and direct application of basic number, money and measures to situations very similar to those they have encountered in school mathematics. Occasionally somewhat unrealistic school mathematics problems are identified as being possible real-life situations:

When we went down to the shop the other day Paul was beginning to buy three Refreshers and I said hang on a minute Paul because he was only allowed to spend 30p and they were 12p each and I added them all up and I said that's 36p and he said mum won't mind if I spend 6p extra and I did 12 times 3 is 36. (Denise)

In the same terms the children identify basic number, money and measures as being potentially useful in future life:

> You may have to measure things up when you go to college, and the more you learn at school the better job you'll get. (Daniel)

This is distinct from the Craftsperson because the context of application is less flexible, being like school problems rather than real everyday problems. The latter are more evident in the Craftsperson conceptualisation.

Conception 3: Performer

In this conception children see mathematics as being used to put on a show, to perform and to entertain. In these situations it is always a direct repetition of the practised 'act'. This is distinct from the Labourer conception because the purpose of the direct repetition is to perform and entertain rather than complete mathematical work or tests.

Conception 4: Craftsperson

The children identify simple application in measures and money in a variety of everyday contexts. The focus is on expert tool use:

> Dad has put in a new carpet in Helen's room and I helped dad measure it all up and we had to measure really carefully so that there would be no gaps in the carpet. If you want to find the perimeter of a room you can do one side and then another side and work out the rest. That's what Mr Norman told us. Dad told the people at the carpet shop so they could get the right measurement for Helen's room. (Barbara)

The children also show evidence of a wider view of number, for example, they know when to use multiplication:

> It's like when you want to make things bigger, say five times bigger, so if it's three then five times bigger is 15, and if it's four centimetres then five times bigger is 20 centimetres, so to make a picture five times bigger you'd times all the measurements by five. (Ben)

This differs from Mechanic because with the Craftsperson it is understanding which leads to use in everyday problems rather than clues in the layout or wording of school mathematics problems.

Conception 5: Academic

In terms of use, identifying patterns and generalising are seen as separate strategies and skills that can be applied in other tasks and contexts:

> I have used these ideas when we have done another sheet, and we've done pattern as well, and I've drawn tables. When playing football games I need to draw out a table. I've used other ideas in a piece of work we did a few days ago when we had to make a formula. (Ben)

The value of describing situations mathematically is also recognised:

> When you look at something then, if you look for patterns and then find a formula, you can say what will happen if it's a bit different, like you've got more trains or cars or something, so it will help you see what will happen. (Ben)

Occurrence of conceptions of mathematics within this study

In 88% of instances in mathematics contexts, high-attainers in mathematics in their final year of primary school indicate that their experiences of mathematics are those described in the 'Labourer', 'Mechanic' and 'Craftsperson' conceptions. In these conceptions, use centres on counting, simple number operations, money and measures. Further, in 72% of instances, these children indicate that their experiences of mathematics are those described in the 'Labourer', 'Mechanic' and 'Performer' conceptions. In these:

use is inflexible, being seen as being a direct repetition of that which has been taught;

use can occur either in further mathematical exercises, in performing or in very similar out of school contexts such as adding money;

when the context is different, clues are often used to determine the approach chosen, rather than understanding. These clues might be inappropriate and mislead.

In only 19% of instances did children indicate that their experiences of mathematics are those described in the 'Craftsperson' conception. In this conception understanding determines the mathematics used, and mathematics is used flexibly in appropriate contexts. Further, there is a very low occurrence of instances of children indicating that they have experienced mathematics as suggested by the 'Academic' conception: as a useful way of describing the world.

Analysis

Kelly's research is a good illustration of 'grounded theory' where data are collected, analysed for patterns of response, and categories created. This extract describes the findings of research based on semi-structured interviews with 11-year-old primary school children.

By examining children's attitudes and understanding of mathematics we can begin to gain knowledge of the influence and effect of the application of the policies Brown is referring to in her extract. Although this is a small sample, it offers a window on children's understanding of the nature of mathematics.

Summarise the models described. For example, the 'Labourer' – superficial knowledge and limited application, tends towards literal interpretation and is dependent on spotting key words. Compare your interpretation with that of a colleague. Then consider some of the children you have taught. Which of the categories would you place them in?

What do the categories tell us generally about how mathematics is currently taught? Is there a link between Brown's point about procedural and conceptual mathematics? Has the style of the National Numeracy Strategy led to a particular type of understanding?

One might link the actions of the Craftsperson with Skemp's relational understanding. Are there other categories which fit with relational or instrumental mathematics? Skemp is keen that children should have a relational approach to mathematics. In practical terms, how could a teacher move children towards this goal?

Personal response

Education is a topic frequently addressed in the media and in government announcements. Consider the most recent decisions and how they affect the functioning of the primary school. The introduction of the National Curriculum (1988), the Curriculum Guidance for the Foundation Stage (2000) and the National Numeracy Strategy have dramatically altered the teaching of mathematics. Think about the way mathematics has been taught to you and the way you teach mathematics. Within the time span of your experience, note what changes have occurred. Reflect on the changes in teaching style, the content of what is taught and where the emphasis lies: on knowledge, skills, strategies, real or theoretical mathematics.

Conclusion

There are people who hold the view that mathematics is the one subject which is free from social and cultural influences. These three extracts are pointers to the fact that mathematics education in the primary school is subject to political ideologies, the views held in society of mathematics as a useful subject and the beliefs of teachers on how it should be taught and where the emphasis should lie. This is reflected in the views that children hold about the nature and uses of mathematics. As a teacher it is important to be aware of the political, social and cultural factors and their influence on curriculum and pedagogy. The nature of primary school mathematics is very different from the view of the nature of mathematics as a theoretical subject. However, the nature of the subject itself needs to be addressed too, as this will lead to effective learning. Skemp initiated a powerful model for us to analyse how children understand mathematics.

2 Teaching children to think mathematically

By the end of this chapter you should have:

- considered **why** mathematics education can be described as teaching children to think mathematically;
- identified **what** it means to teach children to think algebraically as a specific example of mathematical thinking;
- reflected on the relationship between teaching strategies and the way in which children learn **how** to think mathematically.

Linking your learning
- Mooney, C, Fletcher, M, Briggs, M and McCullouch, J (2002) *Achieving QTS. Primary mathematics: teaching theory and practice* (2nd edition). Exeter: Learning Matters, Chapters 8 and 10.

Professional Standards for QTS
1.7, 2.1, 3.1.3, 3.2.3

Introduction

This part of the chapter will reflect on why thinking can be argued to be an important part of mathematics education.

In the introduction to the National Curriculum for Mathematics (1999), Sparrow suggests that mathematics is a way of thinking. Do you agree with this? The report by McGuiness (1999), *From thinking skills to thinking classrooms*, aimed to review and evaluate research into the teaching of thinking in school. It was hoped that the report would help analyse the term 'thinking skills', and explore general patterns in the way in which thinking is currently taught. The focus was on the teaching of thinking skills generally, not just within mathematics.

Consider the following extract from the report.

Extract: McGuiness, C (1999) *From thinking skills to thinking classrooms*. www.dfes. gov.uk/research/data/uploadfiles/RB115.doc

Core concepts in a framework for developing thinking skills
Most attempts to teach thinking are based on some formal analysis of the nature of thinking, but what they are all trying to achieve, irrespective of their precise theoretical foundations, is to develop the person's thinking to a qualitatively higher level. Core concepts have emerged.

- Developing thinking skills is supported by theories of cognition which see learners as active creators of their knowledge and frameworks of interpretation. Learning is about searching out meaning and imposing structure.

- Focusing on thinking skills in the classroom is important because it supports active cognitive processing which makes for better learning. It equips pupils to go beyond the information given, to deal systematically yet flexibly with novel problems and situations, to adopt a critical attitude to information and argument as well as to communicate effectively.

- There is a need to be explicit about what we mean by better forms of thinking and of educating directly for thinking. If students are to become better thinkers – to learn meaningfully, to think flexibly and to make reasoned judgements – then they must be taught explicitly how to do it.

- Several taxonomies of thinking are available. They include some reference to sequencing and sorting, classifying, comparing, making predictions, relating cause and effect, drawing conclusions, generating new ideas, problem solving, testing solutions, making decisions and so on. Some approaches identify multiple intelligences for enhancement – linguistic, logical-mathematical, musical, kinesthetic.

- High quality thinking is emphasised in most approaches and there is a need to design learning tasks which are not routine but have a degree of open-endedness and uncertainty to permit learners to impose meaning or to make judgements or to produce multiple solutions.

- It is important to give learners the time and opportunity to talk about thinking processes, to make their own thought processes more explicit, to reflect on their strategies and thus gain more self-control. Acquiring and using metacognitive skills has emerged as a powerful idea for promoting a thinking skills curriculum.

- Children bring their own conceptions (and misconceptions) into the classroom. New knowledge and alternative strategies for thinking are socially constructed in the classroom not only through informed teacher instruction but through practical activities, dialogue, reflection and discussion with peers and adults. Such socially mediated activities need to be carefully designed from a thinking skills perspective.

- Developing better thinking and reasoning skills may have as much to do with creating dispositions for good thinking as it has to do with acquiring specific skills and strategies. For this reason classrooms need to have open-minded attitudes about the nature of knowledge and thinking and to create an educational atmosphere where talking about thinking – questioning, predicting, contradicting, doubting – is not only tolerated but actively pursued.

- Increasingly it is recognised that developing thinking skills has implications not only for pupils' thinking but for teacher development and teacher thinking as well as for the ethos of schools as learning communities.

Analysis

What are the implications of this report for your own teaching of mathematics? Do you believe that, as the report says, children can be active learners of mathematics? A natural answer would be yes, but it is worth spending some time considering what this actually means. Active learners need time and space to make links between existing understanding and new learning. This requires their teacher to be fully aware of their existing understanding. Children need to make mistakes and evaluate their strategies in a secure but challenging classroom environment. They need confidence to ask their teachers questions. They need to be aware of what, when and how they are learning. Are these elements identifiable in the last lesson you taught?

The report talks of 'high-level thinking'. How would you describe high-level thinking in mathematics? It may be more useful for you to start to analyse what is not high-level mathematical thinking. Rapid recall, say, of multiplication facts is an essential component of mathematical thinking, but is not high-level thinking. Being able to reproduce a procedure for subtracting large numbers but not understanding how it works is not high-level thinking. The report talks about children searching for meaning, going beyond the information given in a task, being systematic yet flexible. These are the sort of skills which are listed in the National Curriculum (1999) in Attainment Target 1, 'Using and applying mathematics'. Ensure that you are fully aware of these requirements.

Is mathematics a form of effective communication, which the report states is a result of teaching children to think? The ability to represent data and to interpret them analytically could be seen as an essential part of thinking and arguing. Confidence and agility with the use of mathematical vocabulary might also be the result of teaching children to think mathematically.

Reflect on the report's findings on the way in which teachers can teach children to think. Teachers often need to act as models of thinkers, just as other areas of mathematics are modelled in the mathematics lesson. The teacher then acts as a coach, thinking aloud slowly and explicitly. Children need opportunities to think through problems, which takes time and space. They also need opportunities to decide how to think through problems, and be given freedom to decide this for themselves. There needs therefore to be a balance between specific modelling of thinking strategies by the teacher, and opportunities for children to make decisions themselves about strategies and methods. A mini-plenary during a lesson can be used to discuss possible methods the children could adopt, after they have had some time to consider possibilities themselves. The plenary of the lesson then acts as a time to compare, reflect on and evaluate thinking strategies. The teaching of thinking needs to provide children with a vocabulary of thinking strategies. For example, if children reach a general statement because they spot a pattern in their results, they need a vocabulary which allows them to be able to say this. Talking through thinking takes time, which may not fall neatly into a daily timetabled mathematics lesson. This sort of discussion also relies on an ethos in the classroom where, as the report states, questioning, predicting, contradicting and doubting are encouraged.

Thinking requires suitable tasks to be set. What sort of activities do you feel allow children to think mathematically? These need to be a rich diet of open-ended and closed tasks which do not always specify a recognised method; non-routine questions which allow children to take risks and search for meaning; and those with too much or not enough information which encourage critical evaluation. Does your teaching encourage children to think in this way?

Personal response

How would you describe mathematical thinking? Is it logical, systematic and powerful? Is it imaginative and creative? Is it cold, fixed, rigid and objective? Does mathematical thinking explore connections, reach generalisations, provide useful statements for everyday life, allowing situations to be investigated, resulting in intriguing patterns and relationships?

If you were asked to describe the aims of mathematics education, what would you include? You might think mathematics education is to do with such things as:

- providing children with confidence in mathematics;
- encouraging in children a rich understanding of mathematical ideas;
- equipping children with a set of procedures and rapid recall of facts to solve problems;
- giving children a fascination for mathematics;
- teaching children to think mathematically.

Does the practice of teaching mathematics in the classroom reflect this balance of aims? Consider the learning objectives of the last lessons you taught or observed in school. Were these to do with providing the children with opportunities to think? You may find that there is more emphasis on teaching children to remember and perform a procedure than to think for themselves. Discuss your views with a colleague.

An example: algebraic thinking

This part of the chapter will reflect on pre-algebraic thinking processes as a specific example of mathematical thinking.

What are your memories of algebra? Many people remember pages of exercises, requiring the use of a remembered procedure, perhaps collecting x and y terms and simplifying equations which contained letters. There may be memories of anxiety caused by the lack of context and understanding, and therefore a need to rely on a memory of the procedure. One lesson or part of a lesson missed or not understood might have meant failure in the following exercises. Other people might have more positive memories, having enjoyed the level of success gained from being able to understand or remember the procedure, and the ability to apply it repeatedly to examples.

The manipulation of symbols is a small part of algebra but one which is often remembered by adults. Algebra is difficult to define but involves expressions of generality.

Therefore powerful statements about numbers, data and shapes can be formulated and investigated. For example, algebra might allow us to express and predict the growth of leaves on a plant, how a number sequence will continue, whether odd numbers added to even numbers give odd totals, or how many vertices a 3D shape will have.

The ability to express generalisations with algebra often involves using letters to represent variables. Algebra can therefore be seen as a language or a set of notation tools. The generalisations and use of letters in equations are often abstract. This aspect of algebra can result in children lacking understanding and relying instead on remembered procedures. However, the approach at primary school is to explore the processes which lead to generalisations, keeping these general statements firmly within a context. Proving why generalisations are true is not formally part of the primary curriculum. However, teaching at primary level can encourage children to ask why general rules are true, why patterns exist and to give some convincing arguments even if these are expressed informally with everyday language or pictures instead of symbols and equations.

The next section will lead you to reflect in detail on the place of one aspect of early algebraic thinking in the primary curriculum, that of general statements. In order to engage with this idea, try the following activity.

- Make a $3 \times 3 \times 3$ cube out of smaller 1-unit cubes.

- How many small cubes did you use?

- Imagine dipping it in paint.

- How many of the small cubes have no faces painted?

- How many of the small cubes have one face painted?

- How many of the small cubes have two faces painted?

- How many of the small cubes have three faces painted?

- How many of the small cubes have four faces painted?

- How many of the small cubes have five faces painted?

- How many of the small cubes have six faces painted?

- Investigate for a $4 \times 4 \times 4$ cube and try to predict the answers for other sizes of cubes.

Reflect on your response to this investigation:

- Which problem-solving or investigative strategies did you use?

- Do these appear on the Programme of Study for mathematics or the statements of attainment for Attainment Target 1, 'Using and applying mathematics', in the National Curriculum for Mathematics (1999)?

- Were you methodical in your approach? For example, did you consider a $1 \times 1 \times 1$ cube, a $2 \times 2 \times 2$ cube, a $3 \times 3 \times 3$ cube, a $4 \times 4 \times 4$ cube? Did you list your results, perhaps in some sort of table, in order to spot a pattern?

- Did or could you use this pattern to predict the results for larger cubes?

- Could you state a generalisation perhaps for the number of small cubes which have three faces painted on a cube larger than $2 \times 2 \times 2$? Or could you state a generalisation about the number of small cubes which never get painted in any large cube?

- Did you discuss this investigation with anyone else? How useful is discussion and collaboration?

This type of investigation, although perhaps more at your own level, is an example of an activity that allows children to explore how generalisations can be found within a context which they can visualise and manipulate. An important role of the primary curriculum is to provide contexts for children to use methodical examples to generate number and shape patterns. They can then discuss what is the same and different about the items in the pattern. Young children may spend time simply saying what they see, developing appropriate vocabulary and speaking and listening skills. This leads to an investigation between items in the pattern, and between items in the pattern and their position in the pattern. Children can then describe these patterns in words and pictures, and can use their descriptions to predict further items in the sequence. They can articulate these patterns as general statements in informal language, pictures or even symbols.

This process of using patterns to formulate general statements is one which mathematicians themselves go through, and the initiation of children into this type of thinking can be argued to be an important part of the teaching of mathematics.

Evidence of children's pre-algebraic thinking

The research in the following extract analysed the responses of 11-year-olds to the given Standard Assessment Task question. A sample of 451 scripts from the 2001 Key Stage 2 tests were made available by the Mathematics Test Development Team at the Qualifications and Curriculum Authority (QCA). This sample consisted of roughly a third each of levels 3, 4 and 5. The research considered the successful and unsuccessful strategies recorded by the children in the test in order to explore and identify the most effective thinking strategies.

Extract: Houssart, J and Evans, H (2003) 'Approaching algebra through sequence problems: Exploring children's strategies'. *Research in Mathematics Education*, **5:** **pp197–214.**

23. Here is a sequence of patterns made from squares and circles:

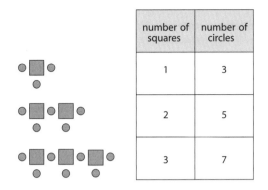

	number of squares	number of circles
	1	3
	2	5
	3	7

The sequence continues in the same way.

Calculate how many **squares** there will be in the pattern which had **25 circles**.

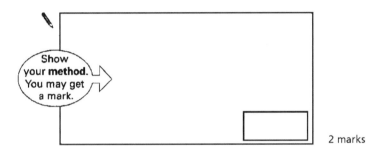

Show your **method.** You may get a mark.

2 marks

Comparison of strategies

It is difficult to define a 'best strategy' for this problem. Using the relationship between the numbers of circles and squares can be seen as the most sophisticated method and would certainly be preferable in the case of a 'far generalisation'. However in this case, some children applying the 'relationship' approach did so the wrong way round and arrived at an incorrect answer. Although 13 children arriving at the correct answer showed some evidence of using a relationship, 9 children apparently applied the relationship the wrong way, arriving at the answer 51.

The drawing approach could be seen as the least sophisticated, but most reliable. However for some children, there is a suggestion that drawing the shapes may have aided their understanding of the relationship. In some cases this was suggested by gaps in the drawing, indicating that children may have added one square and two accompanying circles. This can be seen in another example where the drawing is also accompanied by a statement of the relationship.

However, the use of diagrams was not as foolproof as might be imagined, as some children drew an incorrect pattern. This was particularly the case for children who thought the pattern was three circles round every square and therefore drew that.

As well as accuracy, strategies can also be considered in terms of whether they helped children see the structure of the pattern, though this is not something easy to determine from a written answer. There is a suggestion that some children making correct use of drawings became more aware of the structure of the pattern as they drew.

Implications for teaching

Our findings suggest a wealth of solutions provided by children. Teachers might want to capitalise on this by encouraging a whole class to work on problems such as this and share their solutions.

We have also noted some common errors, which teachers may wish to be aware of. Some of these are likely to occur in any linear generalisation problem. The error of applying the relationship the wrong way is likely to occur only when children are asked for an inverse, as in this problem. One approach to incorrect answers is to return to the stages offered by Mason *et al* (1985): seeing a pattern; saying a pattern; recording a pattern and testing formulations. It seems that many children would be helped by encouragement to carry out the fourth stage. This could mean checking that the relationship or pattern suggested applies to all the diagrams already provided, not just one. It could be extended to include further examples.

Analysis

Many successful answers to the question seemed to use a drawing strategy; for example, drawing enough squares to reach 25 circles. This might be generally considered a low-level thinking skill, but was appropriate in this case where the question required the children to consider a relatively low number of squares. Therefore there was a manageable amount of drawing. This is called a 'near generalisation' by the researchers, where asking how many squares for, say, 99 circles would be a 'far generalisation'.

Some successful answers involved completing a table of results, which was indeed suggested by the question itself. When drawing the table, most children worked down the results, spotting a pattern between each consecutive number of circles. Again, given that the question asked about a near generalisation, it was possible to extend the pattern to 25 circles. A higher level of thinking would be to look at the relationship between squares and circles, and presenting, if informally, a generalisation. Some children attempted this successfully; for example, showing they understood that for every square there were two new circles. The pattern starts with a single circle, so it is possible to find the answer by subtracting 1 from 25 for this starting circle and dividing 24 by 2. Others worded the relationship incorrectly as the inverse, getting the answer of 51. It seems that children tend to find it more accessible to find and describe patterns in numbers rather than to describe relationships between numbers and their position in the pattern. For further reading on this, see Nunes and Bryant (1996). A common error evident in the children's responses was to assume from the second diagram that as two squares have five circles, then 10 squares would have 25 circles. The researchers call this thinking the 'whole object method'. How would you explain to the children that this is incorrect?

The extract suggests that it is important for teachers to model the thinking through of relationships and patterns in tabled results such as these, spending time describing patterns, looking at the relationship between the item and its position in the pattern, and using these to make generalisations and to explore relationships.

The relationship between teaching strategies and how children learn to think mathematically

This part of the chapter will look at the specific teaching strategy of the management of classroom talk and its relationship with the way in which children learn to think mathematically.

Extract: Pratt, N (2002) 'Mathematics as thinking'. *Mathematics Teaching,* **181: 34–7.**

'That's fascinating, but what I want you to see is …'

If you have ever found yourself saying these words then it is likely that, like all teachers, you may be stuck between the rock of encouraging children's thinking and the hard place of trying to develop learning in a particular direction. In the context of the national numeracy strategy the tension can be seen as being between instructions for planning teaching on the one hand and the recommendation for carrying this out on the other. In respect of planning, the claim is that, 'better numeracy standards occur when … the teaching programme is based on identified learning objectives, and is planned thoroughly, to ensure … good progression throughout the school'; regarding implementation, one should use interactive teaching, 'a two-way process in which pupils are expected to play an active part by answering questions, contributing points to discussions, and explaining and demonstrating their methods to the class'. Clearly this represents a potential dilemma, for if one believes that children will learn best when *what* they should learn is detailed in advance, then it becomes problematic when, as it always does, children begin to think about 'something else' as the teaching and learning takes place.

My starting point for considering this dilemma is an assertion: that we want children not just to engage *in* mathematical thinking, but to come to view mathematics *as* thinking. From this perspective, though mathematics of course involves the development of knowledge and practical skills, it is *essentially* about trying to make 'mental sense' of ideas in ways which are coherent and consistent by thinking in particular ways. The numeracy strategy's call for children to contribute to this sense-making is based (presumably – though it is not made explicit) on a belief that we learn most effectively with other people and that *talk* is the primary vehicle for doing so. What I intend to explore here is how, as teachers, we tend to control the flow of children's talk, often to the extent that they cease to be able to become a genuine part of any interaction and how, if we wish to change this, we might profitably reconsider a few of our teaching strategies.

What sort of interaction do we want?
Interaction can, of course, take many forms but I limit myself here to interaction in the form of talk. If we wish to encourage children to make sense of mathematical ideas by thinking and talking, what kinds of thinking and talking do we wish to foster? Mercer

proposes three 'ways of talking and thinking': disputational talk, cumulative talk and exploratory talk. The first of these 'is characterised by disagreement and individualised decision-making'; the second is talk 'in which speakers build positively but uncritically on what the other has said'. However, in exploratory talk people engage in constructive criticism of each others' ideas and,

> knowledge is made more publicly accountable and reasoning is more visible in the talk. Progress then emerges from the eventual joint agreement reached.

It is this last form of talk that seems to me to be what the national numeracy strategy is hoping for in its description of 'whole class interaction'. Knowledge which is publicly accountable might also be shared more readily and reasoning which is visible might be more likely to 'make sense' to children. However, in practice, talk is all too often no better than cumulative with the teacher controlling what is acceptable and what he or she thinks should be said in order to accumulate a 'correct' picture of the idea under discussion. This brings us back to the dilemma outlined above: that the national numeracy strategy encourages a view of mathematics as interactive, but simultaneously as a progressive series of ideas to be acquired under the control of the teacher. In so doing, teachers are recommended to 'involve pupils interactively through carefully planned questioning' and to 'ask pupils to offer their methods and solutions to the whole class for discussion'. Such recommendations are easy enough to make but harder to fulfil. What follows is intended to address this to some extent by both considering the dilemmas involved and offering some simple starting points for resolving them.

Forms of 'thought control'
Twenty-five years ago, when primary teaching was under the influence of a very different set of (Plowdenesque) values than it is today, Edwards and Mercer identified a set of actions which they claimed 'may foster or hinder the development of common (ie, joint) knowledge in the classroom'. My own observations suggest that little seems to have changed despite the changes in values. The list below illustrates some of the teaching actions that, I believe, can potentially hinder thinking in the mathematics classroom, especially where they are done habitually. However, I emphasise that each can also have a positive teaching effect in another context. I invite you therefore to consider them in the light of your own practice and to ask the question how each one might affect the way your children think about mathematics. What happens when you:

- ask a child to explain his or her solution to a problem/calculation without this being an opportunity for other children to explore it in relation to their own; ie the explanation is simply for its own(er's) sake?
- ask more than one child to explain the same problem/calculation without contrasting them?
- support a child with his or her answer by:
  - interrupting it and/or finishing it off in your own words?
  - reinterpreting what had been said to mean something different?
  - ignoring the whole answer because it does not match the teaching point?
  - ignoring the whole answer for fear that it could not be understood sufficiently by others?
  - ignoring elements of the answer in order to refocus it on something new?

- repeating the answer, emphasising certain elements of it and thereby changing the meaning?
- using value judgements ('good', 'I'm not sure about that', quizzical looks etc.) thereby endowing certain aspects of the answer with special significance?

Analysis

To what extent do your choices of teaching strategies present your views of mathematics itself? The following quote from Bills *et al.* (2004) explores the impact of teachers' questions on how mathematics is perceived by children.

A learner's experience in the classroom frames the view she will have about the subject. If she is asked closed questions with attention only to right answers, then getting an answer, any answer, will become the aim of mathematics; if all that is asked is that the work is neat and tidy, then neatness and completion will become the aims of mathematics; if she is asked to express her thoughts about a concept, then expressing her thoughts will become the aim; if she is asked to think, to develop relationships and structures, to compare them to, and eventually express them in, conventional forms, then these will become the aims of mathematics. The questions and prompts used, and the responses to these which are accepted become the model of mathematical behaviour for the learner. It follows that if pupils are embedded in a context in which a rich variety of question types are being used, they are likely to pick up a sense of the subject as a richly embroidered fabric.

Personal response

What are the implications of this quote for your own teaching? Ask a colleague to record the types of questions you ask, or study your lesson plans for evidence of question types. Do you present this rich diet?

Reflect on Edwards and Mercer's framework for analysing talk in the classroom. Is this a useful framework to reflect on the balance of types of talk in your lessons? What is the ideal balance between disputational, cumulative and exploratory talk? What is the balance in your classroom? Does this vary as to the type of lesson, its objectives, and the position of the lesson in a series studying a particular topic? For example, is the type of talk at the beginning of a week's work on, say, fractions different from the type of talk at the end of the week?

Explore the final three points of the extract. When exactly is it appropriate to adopt these strategies, and when do these strategies limit children's thinking? For example, do you ask children to explain their strategies in mathematics without investigating these further with the whole class? This might be a useful form of assessment from time to time, but the article argues that strategies need to be valued, evaluated, contrasted, compared, explored and investigated to allow thinking to take place.

Discuss your views with a colleague.

Consider the learning objectives you use in the classroom, whether specified by the National Numeracy Strategy, Unit Plans, published mathematics schemes, or school's medium-term plans. Do you feel there is a tension between these learning objectives and the idea of teaching children to think mathematically? Is your teaching balanced between the need to teach children extremely useful facts, procedures, vocabulary and the need to allow children time to think?

Conclusion

This chapter has guided you through a series of reflections on the place of mathematical thinking in your classroom. The importance of pattern in pre-algebraic thinking has been considered in detail. Continued reflection on the impact of your teaching strategies on children's thinking will help you to apply some of the ideas here to your own teaching. However, your teaching of mathematical thinking depends on your ability to think mathematically. Engaging and reflecting on your response to investigations such as the painted cube activity presented here enable you to identify and evaluate thinking processes and to act as a coach to children as they begin to think mathematically.

3 Number: learning to count and understand place value

By the end of this chapter you should have:

- reflected on **why** children find learning to count difficult;
- considered **what** elements are involved in becoming a successful number user;
- identified **how** teachers can help children to learn to count and use place value to support calculation.

Linking your learning

- DfEE (1999) *The National Curriculum.* London: DfEE Publications, Attainment Target 2.
- Mooney, C, Fletcher, M, Briggs, M and McCullouch, J (2002) *Achieving QTS. Primary mathematics: teaching theory and practice* (2nd edition). Exeter: Learning Matters, Chapters 2, 10 and 11.

Professional Standards for QTS
1.7, 2.1, 3.3.2

Introduction

It often appears to adults that learning to count is an easy process. It is something that most of us learnt so long ago we cannot remember learning how to do it, or not being able to do it. Similarly, the understanding and use of place value is integral to much of the daily use we make of numbers. To become successful users of numbers and successful calculators, we need to be able to count efficiently and accurately. A deeper understanding of the number system, through place value, allows us to calculate with confidence. This chapter will explore some of the processes and concepts involved in learning to count and develop an understanding of place value.

The principles involved in learning to count

The following extract looks more closely at the elements involved in being able to count accurately and reliably.

Extract: Montague-Smith, A (1997) *Mathematics in nursery education*. London: David Fulton, Chapter 1, pp6–9.

Developing counting skills in the nursery
From the mass of evidence of how children learn to count, Gelman and Gallistel (1986) produced five principles which state the counting concepts which children need to

acquire to become proficient at counting. These are:

- the one-one principle;
- the stable-order principle;
- the cardinal principle;
- the abstraction principle;
- the order-irrelevance principle.

The one–one principle

This is the matching of counting words to the items to be counted. Children need to understand that each number word can only be used once and that every item in the set must be assigned a number word, or tagged. To do this effectively, the number words need to be used in order and the items to be counted partitioned into two sets, a set of items which have already been tagged and those to be tagged.

The stable-order principle

As well as assigning a counting word to each item in the set to be counted, children must learn to repeat the counting words in order. Counting words in the English language have no recognisable pattern to them until fourteen, fifteen, sixteen.... Learning to count involves rote learning of the counting names and from one to thirteen there is no discernible pattern in English and these words will be learnt, in order, by rote. The pattern within each decade is recognisable, that is, twenty-one, twenty-two... and then each new decade name, thirty, forty, must be learnt. As children become proficient counters to ten, then twenty, they sometimes continue to count without recognising the decade change as the following example of Liam's counting (5 years 5 months) shows:

> one, two, three ... eighteen, nineteen, twenty, twenty-one ... twenty-nine, twenty-ten, twenty-eleven, twenty-twelve ... twenty-twenty.

At first children will 'chant' numbers, perhaps learnt through number rhymes and stories, and this chant will appear to have no meaning. Gradually, the order of the words takes on meaning and becomes related to items to be counted. Children begin to realise that the order of the counting words is always the same and that in order to count they must reproduce this order. This is the stable-order principle.

The cardinal principle

The final number in the count, that is the cardinal number of the set, represents how many are in the set. In order to say how many in a set, children need to recognise that the last number in their count represents how many there are in the set, so that as well as touching and counting one-one, using the counting names in order and consistently, they must be able to stop on the last number of the count and recognise that as how many there are. The cardinal principle is dependent upon the one-one and the stable-order principles and is a later stage of development.

These first three principles are called the 'how to count' principles (Gelman and Gallistel, 1986). Bird (1991) defines four co-ordination skills in counting:

- using a counting word for each object;
- counting each object just once;
- stopping the count at the correct point;
- using the counting words in the correct order, starting and stopping at the right place.

To this should be added:

- understanding that the last number in the count represents the cardinal number of the set.

The abstraction principle

This principle states that the how-to-count procedure can be applied to any counting situation. Children can count any set, whether it is made up of similar objects (such as toy cars) or unlike objects (such as a doll, ball, plate, and shoe). In counting a set of similar objects a child might say 'There are four cars'. Here the child is able to name the set as cars. However, where the objects are unlike they will need to find a common property of the set, such as 'There are four things'. Adults know that anything can be counted, whether it can be seen or imagined, and anything can be grouped together to be counted. Gast (1957, in Gelman and Gallistel, 1986) suggests that three and four year olds can only count things which are identical with each other and that any variation in the material, by colour for example, causes a break in the ability to count. This argument has fed the notion that pre-number activities must be based upon sorting and classifying activities. However, it is now thought that practical experience of counting is what determines the child's development and so children should be encouraged to count any set which they have compiled, and which they see as countable.

The order-irrelevance principle

Given a set of a toy car, lorry, motorbike, bus and fire engine, arranged in a line, adults know that it is quite acceptable to call the car 'one' on the first count and the lorry 'one' on the second. In other words, the order in which items are counted does not affect the cardinal number of the set. Young children will not have this understanding and will need experience of counting the sets in different orders to begin to appreciate that the order of counting does not affect the cardinal number of the set. Once this fact has been understood children are said to know the following (Gelman and Gallistel, 1986):

- something counted is a thing, not a one or a two;
- the counting numbers are used as counting tags for the objects to be counted, and once the count is over, they no longer belong to those objects;
- in whatever order the objects are counted, the cardinal number of the set remains the same.

Analysis

Theory about early understanding of number has shifted substantially in the past 30 years. At one time dominated by a Piagetian viewpoint of initiating mathematics through classifying and set work, there is now a strong lobby of belief that counting forms the major starting point for children learning mathematics. This has gained much support through the advent of the National Numeracy Strategy but there is a current move to recognise that early mathematics is derived from real contexts and is more than learning about number. This broadening of the mathematics curriculum is gaining ground in Foundation Stage teaching. Most importantly, recognition of the stages of number development have not been lost, and the work of Fuson (1982), Gelman and Gallistel (1986) and Hughes (1986) significantly underpin early number teaching.

As can be seen from the extract, learning to count is no simple feat. There are many processes at work and a number of places where the counting can go wrong. This has implications for teachers of young children, as opportunities are needed to explore and practise all of the elements that constitute counting. Many parents will bring their children to the Nursery or Reception class confidently saying that their child can count, but often they mean that the children can recite the number names in order, i.e. they have acquired the stable-order principle explained above (Gelman and Gallistel, 1986). This is perhaps the most commonly practised element of mathematics in the home and the number names come into many nursery rhymes and early songs that children may sing with their parents. It is worth noting that many such songs count backwards (e.g. 'Ten green bottles', 'Ten in the bed'), and songs that count forwards, which children need to master first, are more difficult to think of. Another dimension to consider is the relationship between home and school mathematics. As Munn (1997) found in her research of pre-schoolers' beliefs about counting, children see counting at home as a play activity with oral emphasis and little quantity value attached.

Despite this being one of the more readily acquired principles, one cannot assume that children can identify the number before a given number without beginning to count at one, indicating a form of rote learning which can be likened to Skemp's description of instrumental learning (see Chapter 1). A further aggravation to learning is the idio-syncratic nature of the English number names. Children generally learn the numbers from 1 to 20 and then the decade numbers (20, 30, 40,). The pattern is mostly repetitive but there are early anomalies in the teen numbers which do not follow any verbal pattern, with 'eleven' and 'twelve' bearing no aural relationship to any other numbers. Countries such as Korea have a distinct advantage when counting 'eight, nine, ten, ten-one, ten-two', etc.

Other counting principles are also prone to difficulty and error. When counting sets of items, some young children reach the wrong total for a number of reasons. To achieve the one–one principle children need to be able to co-ordinate one number name to each item. Misconceptions include counting objects twice, using the two syllables of 'seven' to count two objects, failing to realise the counting rhyme links to the objects, or even failing to stop counting. The counting process needs to develop to deal with representations of quantity in single objects such as coins and graphs, as well as linking words and quantity to symbols. All these bring other levels of complexity to the devel-opment of early number understanding which can be explored in some of the recommended further reading.

Personal response

Listen to young children counting. Where do they make errors in saying the number names? Think of some counting activities which would support each of the counting principles explained by Montague-Smith.

Place value

Once children can count small numbers and have appreciated the pattern of the English counting system, then theoretically they can count to any number they wish and the ideas of 'one more' and infinity may begin to form in their minds. Often around this time children will want to know about the biggest number and will be interested in the words that indicate large numbers, such as million, billion, trillion, even making up their own number names.

Once the number 10 is reached, place value becomes a factor. It is interesting to observe how long children sustain a counting-on system in addition and when they are able to switch confidently to partitioning two- and three-digit numbers to deal with addition and subtraction. The concept of place value has a long history in primary mathematics syllabi. The idea of needing to understand the value of digits in two-, three- and more-digit numbers is well established and the concept of the 100s column, 10s column and units or 1s column appears in many published mathematics schemes. This is particularly true of schemes published before the introduction of the National Numeracy Strategy (1999) as the use of the standard written algorithm for addition, subtraction and multiplication will only work if the calculation is set out with the correct digits in the correct columns (see Chapter 4).

Haylock and Cockburn (1989) discuss the importance of understanding place value as a basis for calculation work. They highlight the need to make *connections between symbols, language, concrete experiences and pictures* to aid the children's understanding of this concept. They also discuss the concept of 'exchange', for in order to understand place value it is necessary to understand that 10 units can be exchanged for one 10, ten 10s can be exchanged for one 100, and so on.

Before reading the following extract, work out the answers to the questions: 25 plus 23 and 46 – 24. Note whether you use a strategy where you count on or whether you add 20 and 40 and 3 and 6. You might use a strategy similar to a written response where units and tens are added separately as if they are single digits. This response is one based on knowledge of the way place value behaves.

Extract: Thompson, I and Bramald, R (2002) *An investigation of the relationship between young children's understanding of the concept of place value and their competence at mental addition.* **Funded by the Nuffield Foundation 2000–2002, Final report April 2002. University of Newcastle.**

Discussion

The Venn diagram showed clearly that only **four** of the 91 successful calculators could be said to have shown an excellent understanding of place value by dint of the fact that they successfully answered both question 8a and 9. This obviously means that 87 (96%)

of them were considered not to have achieved this level of understanding, and yet they were still able to perform a two-digit calculation successfully using partitioning and recombining – a procedure that would appear to depend substantially on a thorough understanding of place value. But if these children do not understand place value then what is it that they do understand?

The ability to perform such calculations must require a basic understanding of certain aspects of the structure of the number system and specific relationships within that structure. The findings reported earlier on the 'face value' task (question 6: 'the 1 in 16 stands for 10 cubes') give the impression that the children in this study have a very good understanding of place value compared with children of a similar age in other studies in other countries (70% success rate compared with 44%), and yet only 4% of them successfully answered both question 8a and question 9. There is clearly an important difference between the aspects of place value probed by these two questions and those probed by the 'face value' task.

The results of this study show that it is possible for children to know that 16 comprises one ten and six ones without their being aware of the column structure of the notation system used for written numbers. The children in this study are likely to have learned about 16 being ten and six from the substantial work on partitioning and recombining of numbers recommended throughout National Numeracy Strategy publications. They will probably have recognised that 16 seen as 10 and 6 is an easy partition to remember, and will have developed an implicit appreciation of the effect on the written form of a number when 10 is added to any single digit number. They are also likely to have learned that the 2 in 25 means 'twenty' because of the way the number is said or read. However, it does not necessarily follow that these same children will be aware that the 2 is in the tens column and therefore means 'two tens'. in this study only 14 (15%) of the 91 successful calculators used a phrase like 'two and two make four' when adding 25 and 23, whereas the remaining 77 (85%) said 'twenty and twenty make forty'. Given that half of these 14 children came from just two different schools, it seems likely that they had been taught a formal calculation algorithm. It is important to note that not a single child explained their working as 'two tens and two tens make four tens'.

Thompson (2000) has demonstrated that children's informal mental and written calculation strategies, as described in the literature, rely substantially on what he calls *quantity value*: the understanding that a two-digit number such as 47 can be partitioned into 'forty' and 'seven' and that the partitioned parts can be operated upon separately. The research reported here would appear to strengthen his argument that there is an important distinction to be made between knowing that 73 is 'seventy' and 'three' and knowing that it is 'seven tens' and 'three units'. This distinction lies at the heart of his argument that what we have up to now called place value should be seen as comprising two separate concepts: *quantity value* and *column value*. The findings of this study suggest that an understanding of the former develops before the latter, and lends support to the argument for delaying the teaching of tens and units column value – until later in the curriculum. According to Thompson (1999) this teaching need not take place until such time as children are to be taught the standard algorithms for the basic operations. It is interesting to note that the Netherlands was the most successful European country in the primary mathematics section of the Third International Mathematics and Science Survey (Keys et al,1996), and yet the Dutch make little or no mention of place value in what might be considered their equivalent of our National Curriculum (Freudenthal Institute, 2001).

When children are adding twenties in this study their focus of attention is the oral/aural aspect of number rather than the written aspect. Recent psychological research suggests that these might be processed in different parts of the brain. Donlan (1998) writing about issues in current 'brain-based' research argues that

> ... there is general acknowledgement that numerical information processing, in the adult at least, involves verbal and non-verbal systems that may operate independently. (p. 257).

The research reported here suggests that this may well also be true for children. The implication is that teachers and children need to spend a substantial amount of time developing links between these verbal and non-verbal systems.

Ross (1985) has argued in her stage model of place value understanding that children's appreciation that the tens digit represents sets of ten objects is contemporaneous with the acquisition of the concept of the whole being the sum of the parts. Sinclair's (1992) data suggest that the latter is acquired well before the former, and the results of this study add weight to her argument in that 63% of the sample correctly added two two-digit numbers using partitioning: a procedure that demands an appreciation not only of the fact that the whole is the sum of the parts, but that the separate parts can be added and a new whole constructed from these new parts. Of these 91 successful calculators only 4% were in the 'excellent understanding of place value' category. The weakness in Ross's (1985) argument probably stems from her failure to distinguish between knowing that the 2 in 23 stands for 'twenty' and knowing that it stands for 'two tens', i.e. between 'quantity value' and 'column value'.

In 1985 Hilary Shuard stated that:

> … in the present curriculum the introduction of ideas of place value is probably postponed for too long for many children … (p 114)

The findings of this study suggest that in the present curriculum ideas of place value, *at least with regard to the aspect of column value*, might be introduced too early for many children. Further research should investigate the possibility that the teaching of column value so early as is still done in many English and American schools, contributes towards both countries' relatively poor performance in the number section of international mathematics surveys.

Analysis

This extract is taken from a research report in which Thompson and Bramald studied 144 children in Years 2–4 from eight primary schools. The children were asked a range of questions relating to the value of digits in two-digit numbers and asked to perform some simple calculations. The extract is the discussion of their research and draws out some interesting ideas. Within this research Thompson and Bramald make a distinction between two aspects of place value: column value and quantity value. They explain *column* value as understanding that the '3' in 34 stands for 3 tens and *quantity* value as understanding that the '3' in 34 stands for 30.

Personal response

Reflect now on your answers to the calculations you completed before you read the extract. Did you use your knowledge of place value to help you answer these questions? If so, do you think you used column or quantity value to help you?

Thompson and Bramald conclude their research by stating that the idea of place value, particularly in respect of column value, *might be introduced too early for many children*. In your experience of working with children, do you think this is true?

If the importance of learning place value is to support calculation, then it appears that different aspects of place value are associated with different methods. With the current emphasis on mental calculation strategies discussed in Chapter 4, is this an argument in support of Thompson and Bramald's point, to teach children the quantity value aspect of place value only? Understanding of the quantity value supports partitioning, which is a key factor in successful mental calculation. Explore some mental and written calculations with colleagues and analyse which aspects of place value have been used. Anghileri (2000) discusses the concept of 'number sense', which she defines as being able to work flexibly to solve problems and having a feel for numbers. This links with Skemp's (1977) theory of instrumental and relational learning. One might argue that algorithms are a form of instrumental learning, whereas having a 'feel for number' is required for relational learning to take place. Anghileri also argues that the learning of place value should draw on real-life examples and that teachers should use visual resources to help children understand place value so that the children can then use this understanding to support their calculation work. Consider which of the resources available in school best support place value.

Personal response

At school, do you think you were taught the column or quantity aspect of place value? Do you think this has been of use to you as an adult? When calculating, do you use column or quantity place value? Do you think both of these aspects should be taught in school now? Look through the National Numeracy Strategy and trace how counting develops into place value.

Work with some children and ask them what the different digits represent in some two- or three-digit numbers. Compare your findings to Thompson and Bramald's – do the children explain using column value or quantity value in their answers?

Conclusion

There has been good, extensive research into the development of young children's understanding of number. Based on this the National Numeracy Strategy has introduced new approaches to teaching children number. This chapter has focused on two aspects which help us to understand how children begin to develop their number knowledge. Detailed examination of children's understanding of calculation and the number system will lead to better ways of teaching mathematics.

4 Mental and written calculation strategies

By the end of this chapter you should have:

- reflected on **why** mental calculation strategies are such an important strand of today's mathematics teaching;
- considered **what** the links are between mental and written calculation;
- identified **how** the approach taken to calculation will be affected by your own experiences of mathematics.

Linking your learning

- DfEE (1999) *The National Numeracy Strategy.* London: DfEE Publications, Introduction, pp6–8.
- Mooney, C, Fletcher, M, Briggs, M and McCullouch, J (2002) *Achieving QTS. Primary mathematics: teaching theory and practice* (2nd edition). Exeter: Learning Matters, Chapter 9.

Professional Standards for QTS
1.7, 2.1, 3.3.2

Introduction

This chapter will discuss some of the current issues surrounding the teaching of written and mental calculation strategies.

In order to facilitate reflection on your own mental and written methods of calculating, determine the answers to the following problems.

$45 + 35$

$212 - 99$

$185 - 47$

25×5

Reflect on how you found the answers to these questions and make a note for later in this chapter. Your responses to these questions, how confident you felt and the approach you took will largely reflect the teaching of calculation you experienced in your own education.

Which calculation methods should be taught in school?

The debate between written and mental calculation strategies

Extract: Plunkett, S (1981) 'Decomposition and all that rot', in Floyd, A (ed)
Developing mathematical thinking. **pp177–181. London: Addison Wesley.**

How are calculations taught?

In contrast to the diversity of methods people actually use, there is very little variation in the methods taught in schools. At the present moment, it is a fair bet that almost all children in this country are taught standard written algorithms for the four rules of number. By this I mean processes for addition, subtraction, long and short multiplication and division which are laid out something like this:

$$
\begin{array}{cccc}
\begin{array}{r} 5\,7 \\ +_1 3\,8 \\ \hline 9\,5 \end{array} &
\begin{array}{r} {}^4\!\cancel{5}\,{}^1 7 \\ -\,3\,8 \\ \hline 1\,9 \end{array} &
\begin{array}{r} 5\,7 \\ \times\quad 8 \\ \hline 4\,5\,6 \\ {}^{5} \end{array} &
\begin{array}{r} 1\quad 9 \\ 3\overline{|\,5\,{}^2 7} \end{array}
\end{array}
$$

There are minor variations, of course, concerning whether you multiply first by the units or by the tens in long multiplication, and whether the quotient goes above or below the dividend in short division, and there is the relatively major distinction between decomposition and equal additions. But that's about the sum of it. The vast majority of children are taught these methods as the primary way of dealing with whole number (and decimal) calculations; and for the majority, I suspect, these are the *only* methods they are taught.

The nature of standard written algorithms

Why should this be? The reasons lie largely in the nature of these algorithms. It is worth attempting to summarise them.

1   They are *written*, so the calculation is permanent and correctible.
2   They are *standardised*: it is possible to arrange that everyone does the same thing.
3   They are *contracted* in the sense that they summarise several lines of equations involving distributivity and associativity.
4   They are *efficient*. For instance, it's less efficient to add the tens first, because you might need to make a subsequent amendment to their total after you've added the units.
5   They can be *automatic*: they can be taught to, and carried out by, someone who has no understanding of what is happening.
6   They are *symbolic*. One does one's calculations entirely by symbol manipulation, with no reference to the real world, or any other model. At the last stage the answer appears with, usually, no previous approach to it.
7   They are *general* in the sense that they will work for any numbers, large or small, whole or decimal, with few or many digits. This is perhaps their greatest attraction, and it comes from their exploitation of place value.
8   They are *analytic*. They require the numbers to be broken up, into tens and units digits, and the digits dealt with separately.

9 They are *not easily internalised*. They do not correspond to the ways in which people tend to think about numbers.

10 They encourage *cognitive passivity* or suspended understanding. One is unlikely to exercise any choice over method and while the calculation is being carried out one does not think much about why one does it in that way.

Possibly the most significant of these characteristics is the eighth. By breaking a number up into hundreds, tens and units digits, and dealing with these as digits, we develop methods which can be applied to all numbers, however large or small, and which can be applied efficiently. However, such an analytical approach detaches the methods from the area of complete numbers (i.e. numbers not split into digits) where people are more at home. Thus even if the rules can be remembered they are learnt largely without reasons and are not related to other number knowledge. They are far from aiding the understanding of numbers; rather they encourage a belief that mathematics is essentially arbitrary.

As has often been stated, training in these methods may be a good idea it you want to produce clerks, and others, who are quick and accurate at doing large numbers of difficult calculations by hand. Also, teaching these methods leaves you with work which is easy to manage and to mark.

Perhaps a further point should be added to the list above: they are *traditional*. For a lot of non-specialist teachers of mathematics, as for the general public, the four rules of number are the standard written algorithms. Concept and algorithm are equated. So to teach division you teach a method rather than an idea. And the method will be the one you were taught, and in this area, at least, you can perpetuate your own knowledge with some confidence …

The nature of mental algorithms

Work these in your head, or better still ask a child, and try to determine how they were done:

$$57 + 24 \qquad 83 - 69 \qquad 3 \times 24 \qquad 112 \div 4$$

Here are some of the characteristics of mental algorithms. They contrast with those in the list above, but there has been no attempt to match them point for point.

1 They are *fleeting* and often difficult to catch hold of.
2 They are *variable*. From his 80 children, Jones recorded 16 different methods altogether for finding $83 - 26$. Of these, three were standard written algorithms.
3 They are *flexible*, and can be adapted to suit the numbers involved. Do you have different methods for $83 - 79$, $83 - 51$, $83 - 7$?
4 They are *active* methods in the sense that the user makes a definite, if not always very conscious, choice of method and is in control of his own calculations.
5 They are usually *holistic*, in that they work with complete numbers rather than separated tens and units digits, e.g. $4 \times 35 = 2 \times 70 = 140$; 4×28: $4 \times 30 = 120 - 8$, 112.

6 They are frequently *constructive*, working from one part of the question towards the answer, e.g. 37 + 28: 37, 47, 57, 67, 65.

7 They are *not designed for recording* so written down they tend to sprawl, as in the example above. But they can of course be recorded where this is desirable.

8 They *require understanding* all along. A child who gets his mental calculations right almost certainly understands what he is doing. Equally their use develops understanding. But on the other hand they cannot be used to achieve performance in advance of understanding.

9 They are often *iconic.* Either they relate to an icon such as the number line or a number square, or they depend upon serial enunciation as in 32 + 21: 32, 42, 52, 53. in either case some overall picture of the numbers is being used.

10 Often they give an *early approximation* to the correct answer. This is usually because a left-most digit is calculated first, but in the context of complete numbers, e.g. 145 + 37: 175, 182; 34 × 4 = 120, 136.

11 They are *limited* in the sense that they cannot be applied to the most difficult calculations, such as 269 × 23. Nevertheless they are suitable for a greater range of problems than a casual observation of school number work might lead one to suspect.

It is fairly clear that mental methods are the ones to foster if you wish to use and develop children's understanding of number, and any teaching of them would obviously be accompanied by other means to this end. You would have to accept that children would not be able to do calculations before they had a pretty clear idea of what was going on. You would have to be able to provide them with alternative ways of dealing with difficult calculations. And a teacher of these methods would obviously expect a degree of independence and individuality in his pupils.

So teachers, or schools, or society, have a choice in the methods which might be taught, and the choice can be made on the basis of previously determined aims in number education. Either standard written algorithms for efficiency and order and because that is what we have taught for 100 years, or mental algorithms for independence and understanding and because they are the methods people actually use. Or both: 'Ah, mental algorithms are all very well, but they must learn the standard methods sooner or later.' Must they?

Analysis

Reflect on how you found the answers to the calculations in the introduction to this chapter. The questions were deliberately presented in a horizontal format. Would you have used a different method if the calculations had been presented in a vertical format as indicated below?

$$
\begin{array}{cccc}
45 & 212 & 185 & 25 \\
+35 & -99 & -47 & \times 5 \\
\hline
\end{array}
$$

Although this extract was written over 20 years ago, the ideas expressed in Plunkett's writing are current today and underpin many of the ideas on calculation in the National Numeracy Strategy (DfEE, 1999). You will notice from reading the National

Numeracy Strategy that mental calculation is given a high profile and that children are encouraged to always use mental calculation as a first resort when attempting to find an answer to a problem. They should only resort to written calculation if the numbers are too large to cope with mentally. Is this the way you calculate?

Many adults do not feel confident when calculating mentally and resort to written methods, often because these were the methods they were taught at school. Consider Plunkett's comments carefully in the light of your own experience. Consider the roles of memory, success, procedural knowledge and understanding in your own success and that of children you have taught. How effectively do children solve problems which involve calculation? Why do you think the success rate plummets in tests where word problems are involved? Is it sufficient to have procedural knowledge which Skemp would describe as instrumental, or is Skemp's relational knowledge required too? Relate Skemp's view (see Chapter 1) to calculating in context and context-free situations. Analyse why teachers are often unwilling to explain why procedures work. These are the points that Plunkett is drawing to our attention in this extract. He develops these points by arguing that schools should teach mental algorithms in preference to written algorithms as they are more useful to the student in adult life.

Some of the principles behind the mental calculation strategies that are promoted by the National Numeracy Strategy appear to have principles in common with the Dutch RME methods (see Chapter 6). Murphy (2003) states: *The fundamental principle of the approach is to engage in mathematics as human activity.* It is questionable as to whether the way that these mental methods are taught in schools encourages the learning of mathematics as a 'human activity' or as simply as a stepping stone to formal written methods for calculating.

Mental algorithms contrast with written algorithms in a number of ways. When reading these points, reflect on the ways you reached your answers to the above calculations.

1   Mental calculations do not rely entirely on good memory; they rely on an understanding of the number system and of how the numbers interrelate.

The argument here is that if you have an understanding of the number system and the calculation you are trying to perform, there are many ways to reach the answer. Of course some of these are more efficient and therefore less prone to error than others. It would be time-consuming and inefficient to answer the problem 45 + 35 by counting 45 cubes and then 35 cubes and then the whole set of cubes. Nevertheless, if this were the only way you knew how to reach the solution, it could be done this way. This is not the same with standard written algorithms. You need to follow the steps of the procedure, in the correct order, and if you forget there is no fall-back position. This is an example of instrumental understanding (Skemp, 1977), where children memorise a method but an error in the algorithm will generate an incorrect solution. Askew (1993) refers to this as a 'bug'. Once a bug is learnt it will cause the same type of error every time the child attempts that style of calculation. Teachers need to look out for these bugs and analyse them to help children correct their procedures. These bugs are often referred to as 'misconceptions' and are difficult to unlearn.

2 When calculating mentally, the whole number is considered when reading the question. For example, 45 + 35 is read as 'forty-five plus thirty-five'. When presented vertically, often the first thing we read is (starting in the right-hand column) 'five plus five', followed by 'four plus three', plus the 'one we carried', and at no time do we actually look at the whole numbers we are dealing with.

This can be an important point at the end of the calculation, as mental estimation ought to take place. If we have read the whole numbers we are dealing with and have arrived at a ridiculous answer, we are more likely to notice. Again this is not likely to happen with standard written algorithms.

3 Mental calculation strategy can be adapted to fit the purpose.

Reflect on how you calculated 212 – 99 and 185 – 47. If you worked these out mentally you will almost certainly have used two different methods. Most adults will use compensation for the first problem, i.e. they will subtract 100 and then add 1; but they will use a different strategy (usually counting on or a partitioning based strategy) for the second problem. If the questions had been written vertically, you would probably have calculated them with a written method using the same procedure regardless of the question.

Do you agree with the points made above? When presented with these issues, adults fall into two main groups. For some adults, often those who felt they had little success at school mathematics, this is a validation of thoughts they had always had but felt that calculating in this way wasn't 'proper' mathematics and was somehow cheating.

Other adults, often those who feel they were successful at school mathematics, do not understand what all the fuss is about! Having found calculation easy, it can be very difficult to put yourself into the shoes of those who have been unable to learn and apply algorithms (especially written ones). This is a difficulty faced by many teachers. Aubrey (1997) studied the subject knowledge of teachers of children in the Early Years. One of her conclusions was that the teachers' subject knowledge (unlike their knowledge of learning and teaching) was not transformed as they became more experienced practitioners but it depended on 'what the teachers bring to the classroom' (Aubrey, 1997, p160). It follows that to teach calculation effectively, teachers must consider the methods they were taught and consider with an open mind methods that may be new to them.

At the end of the extract Plunkett is suggesting that standard written methods may not ever need to be taught in schools. For 1981 this was quite a revolutionary suggestion. To what extent have we adopted his ideas in the primary mathematics curriculum? Reflecting on the way you calculate as an adult, and thinking about children you have seen calculating in school, do you agree with this view? In the full article he goes on to argue that calculation teaching should be in three stages:

1 the acquisition of mental techniques;

2 the use of calculators;

3 the development of some casual written methods.

Plunkett further argues that there is no place (or need) in today's society for the teaching of standard written methods. Thompson (2003) discusses the learning necessary to move from mental calculation to standard written calculation. He argues that: *this progression is not as natural as it first appears to be, and that more thought needs to be given to, and more research carried out concerning, the links between strategies, both mental/mental and mental/written.* This difficulty is further exemplified in the extract on division strategies that follows.

What strategies do children use to solve division problems?

In the next extract Julia Anghileri reports on research into division strategies. Children were given a division test with context questions and pure calculation ('bare') questions on division. The tests were given twice in the school year, five months apart.

Extract: Anghileri, J (2001) 'Development of division strategies for Year 5 pupils in ten English schools'. *British Educational Research Journal*, 27(1): pp85–103.

Discussion
In between the two tests, all pupils would have had 5 months of additional experience with number work in the classroom. Despite this work, which would usually have included specific teaching of division, improvement in performance was only evident in little over half (52%) of the sample. Many pupils made more errors or missed out more problems in the second test than in the first. In both tests, informal strategies were most often low level and inefficient for the large numbers involved. The most successful strategies involved high level chunking in which pupils used their understanding of number relations in an efficient procedure. This was sometimes undermined by poor structure in the recording and correct working, and poor written recording made it difficult for some pupils to extract an answer.

Progression in the second test to higher level, more efficient informal strategies was less evident than changes to the standard algorithm or mental calculation showing no working. High level chunking, for example, was the most successful strategy in both tests and would appear to be a progressive development from adding and low level chunking but its use did not increase in the second test. This suggests that many children are trying to move directly from a more intuitive inefficient strategy to the most condensed format of the algorithm.

For most pupils, the intervening 5 months between the tests appears to have included work with the standard algorithm for division and the results show that the use of this strategy rises from 38% of all items in test 1 to almost half (49%) in the second test. Half of these attempts led to an incorrect solution due to errors in using the algorithm or inability to complete the procedure. There were considerable difficulties in using it for large numbers with single-digit divisors; for example, only 22% were correct out of 68% who attempted to use the algorithm for the problem $1256 \div 6$. Since many pupils appear to have met only the 'short division' algorithm for single-digit divisors, there were evident difficulties in applying it to problems with a two-digit divisor, although many pupils attempted this.

Where the algorithm was inappropriate, for example $64 \div 16$, many pupils who attempted to use it were unable to change to an informal strategy. Pupils appear to be particularly strongly influenced to use the standard algorithm in preference to an informal strategy where the problems were given no context.

Where the increases in use of the algorithm were largest in the second test, there were decreases in the number of correct answers ($432 \div 15$ and $604 \div 10$) or a very small increase ($64 \div 16$), suggesting that this approach replaced a more successful informal strategy used in the first test. It appears that more attention to the progressive development of more intuitive strategies, e.g. from adding, to adding (or subtracting) small 'chunks', and then larger, more efficient chunks, would give children alternatives to the algorithm, which is evidently difficult to use for many problems. Teachers will need to help children structure their written recording of these intuitive approaches and to move progressively to gain efficiency.

Division by 10 proved difficult in both tests and fewer than half the pupils solved the problems $802 \div 10$ and $604 \div 10$, whether set in context or bare. In the second test, there was a decrease in success from 50% to 45% where the item $604 \div 10$ was changed from context to bare. Introduction of the standard algorithm does not appear to help children to solve such problems yet many have no informal written strategy to support them in such calculations.

Analysis

What implications do the results of this research have for primary teachers teaching division? Anghileri found that the children performed better when the questions were set in a context (see Chapter 5). Beyond the findings about context, Anghileri also states that children appeared to move from informal methods to the standard algorithm or mental calculation with no working shown. Children in the study had varying degrees of success with this. It is also interesting to note that informal strategies were often low level and inefficient for the large numbers involved. How does this finding relate to the points that Plunkett argues for? Why did the children use inefficient mental methods? Of course, there could be many reasons. Plunkett might argue that these children had been moved onto the standard algorithm for division too quickly, before they were ready, and he would argue that they should not have been moved to this strategy at all.

Would these children have been better equipped to tackle these problems if they had been taught to refine their 'chunking' method to enable them to deal with the larger numbers in the questions posed? Anghileri also comments that some of the children who attempted to use informal written methods were let down by their presentation, which often prevented them from finding the correct answer. In the conclusion to this research report Anghileri states that: *Most successful were the strategies that involved an informal procedure using derived facts with some efficiency gains through doubling or chunking.* She goes on to conclude that standard algorithms should not be taught until children's own flexible mental methods are fully developed, and then only if the written method complements and supports the children's own intuitive approaches. In other work, Anghileri (1997) highlights the importance of children being able to share and discuss their strategies as this will: *encourage comparisons between their different methods and may be used to focus on details of language that will be crucial for the precision needed in mathematics.* So not only do children need to be introduced to flexible mental and written methods, but they need the opportunity to make these their own through discussion, comparison and sharing with their peers. In her conclusion Anghileri agrees with the points made by Plunkett, and these are reflected in her research findings, carried out 20 years after Plunkett's article (1981) and two years after the introduction, in 1999, of the National Numeracy Strategy in English schools.

Personal response

Reflect on your own learning of mathematics. When asked to calculate, what is your initial response? Do you begin to calculate mentally; reach for a pencil and paper; reach for a calculator; or do you have another response? Reflecting on the mathematics you learnt at school, were you taught mental methods or standard written algorithms? How well do you think this has equipped you for adult life? Where have you learnt your mental methods (if not at school)? What has prompted you to undertake this learning? Were you successful in school at using the standard written methods you were taught? Why do you think you were successful (or not)? Do you use these methods at all in your adult life? As a result of all of your learning of mathematics, do you think you are confident in the use of number and have 'number sense'?

Ask children in Year 5 some division calculations (in context and out of context). Do they have the same problems that the children in Anghileri's research had? What strategies do they use to attempt the problems? Do you think the National Numeracy Strategy has helped these children to be better at division than previous generations?

What is the order in which calculation is approached in the National Numeracy Strategy? What view is expressed about the use of calculators in the National Numeracy Strategy?

Conclusion

Effective calculation strategies, both mental and written, have been under a lot of scrutiny. The National Numeracy Strategy has adopted a particular approach to the teaching of calculation, which reflects some of the issues raised in the debate. This chapter has looked at the differences between mental and written calculation, which helps us to understand the reasons why adults and children may experience difficulties, and therefore how we might support children to become more successful at calculating.

5 Contexts for children's mathematical learning

By the end of this chapter you should have:

- reflected on **why** children's learning may be more effective when it is set in a meaningful context;
- considered **what** sort of contexts can have an effect on children's achievement in specific tasks;
- identified **how** teachers can help children to understand mathematics in context.

Linking your learning

- Mooney, C, Fletcher, M, Briggs, M and McCullouch, J (2002) *Achieving QTS. Primary mathematics: teaching theory and practice* (2nd edn). Exeter: Learning Matters, Chapters 4 and 12.

Professional Standards for QTS
1.7, 2.1, 3.1.3, 3.2.3

Introduction

This chapter will guide your reflection on why children's learning may be more effective when it is set in contexts which are meaningful for them.

In a study of how children learn about division, Anghileri (2001) found that when Year 5 children were given division problems to complete, they were generally much more successful in answering tasks set in a context such as: 84 pencils have to packed in boxes of 14, how many boxes will be needed? than tasks set without contexts such as: 84 divided by 14. Do you think this is true of all children across the primary phase in all aspects of mathematics?

Extract, from Hughes, M (1986) 'Bridge that gap'. *Child Education*, **63: 15.**

The language of maths
Children start school with a surprisingly impressive range of mathematical abilities. Does this therefore mean they are ready for more formal arithmetic, either in its spoken form 'two and one makes three', or in its written form '2 + 1 = 3' as soon as they arrive at school, if not before?

This prospect would be viewed with considerable alarm by most teachers of young children and quite rightly so. The gap between understanding 'two bricks and one more makes three bricks' and understanding 'two and one makes three' or '2 + 1 = 3' is a large and difficult one for young children to cross. It is of crucial importance that they are able to bridge this gap with a full understanding of what is involved.

The difficulty of moving from the concrete to the abstract is well illustrated by this conversation with Patrick, another four-year-old:

Adult: How many is two and one more?
Patrick: Four.
Adult: How many is two lollipops and one more?
Patrick: Three.
Adult: How many is two elephants and one more?
Patrick: Three.
Adult: How many is two giraffes and one more?
Patrick: Three.
Adult: So how many is *two* and one more?
Patrick: (Looking adult straight in the eye.) Six

Most preschool children, like Patrick, are unable to answer questions like 'What does two and one make?' or 'How many is two and one more?' Indeed, many seem to regard them as if in a foreign language. To a large extent they are correct, in that these questions belong to the unfamiliar language of school mathematics. One four-year-old, Alison, was quite clear about this: she replied that she couldn't answer such questions as she 'didn't go to school yet'.

The language of school mathematics in fact differs in many ways from the ordinary language which children use before they come to school. For example, it makes use of familiar words, such as 'take away' and 'makes', but uses them in an unfamiliar fashion. it also has the peculiar properly that it is frequently not about anything in particular. The difficulties caused by this property emerge very clearly in the following conversation with four-year-old Ram:

Adult: What is three and one more? How many is three and one more?
Ram: Three and what? One what? Letter? I mean number. (We had earlier been playing a game with magnetic numeral and Ram is presumably referring to them here.)
Adult: How many is three and one more?
Ram: One more what?
Adult: Just one more, you know?
Ram: (disgruntled) I don't know.

When they start school, children need to learn and understand the new and difficult language of mathematics. More specifically, they have to learn to translate this unfamiliar language into their own individual understanding of number. They must learn that a statement like 'two plus one equals three' can be represented by the addition of two bricks and one more, or two lollipops and one more, and so on. They must also learn make the opposite translation: that these concrete additions can all be represented formally as '2 + 1 = 3'.

These links between the abstract and the concrete – what I have called translations – are of crucial importance for the full understanding of mathematics. They are so central to the kind of practical problem-solving encouraged in the Cockcroft Report. This was spelled out quite specifically by Cockcroft (para 249): 'Mathematics is only "useful" to the extent to which it can applied to a particular situation, and it is the ability to apply mathematics to a variety situations to which we give the name "problem-solving". However, the solution of a mathematical problem cannot begin until the problem has been translated into the appropriate mathematical terms. This first and essential step presents very great difficulties to many pupils – a fact which is often too little appreciated.'

Indeed, it seems that many children leave school still unable to make these links and with what is often a major gap between their concrete understanding of number and their ability to manipulate the formal symbols of school mathematics.

Analysis

Why did the children in Hughes' study appear to use mathematics more effectively in meaningful settings? Contexts can enable children to manipulate ideas mentally, within a framework. Numbers, for example, are linked to objects, so a fuller understanding of number can be developed. The number 5 can be explored when counting out pencils for children to use at a table, when laying the table for tea in a role-play area of the classroom, when singing rhymes about currant buns and when counting actions such as jumps in a PE lesson. This is an important part of what Skemp (1989) calls relational understanding, and has been discussed in an earlier chapter.

Operations can also be explored in more depth. Not only are children taught how to add, they are taught when to add. The context provides both the reason for adding and the situation to explore the different structures of addition.

Connections can be made with existing knowledge (Askew *et al.*, 1997). Therefore mathematical learning is not isolated. Mathematical vocabulary can be explored using everyday language, investigating meanings, boundaries and negotiating definitions. This allows a mathematical term to be gradually introduced into the child's everyday vocabulary. Atkinson (1992) calls this *making human sense of mathematics*. The contexts may not always be represented physically, and fingers can act as a representation of a concrete context, but the context itself provides the meaning for mathematics.

What sort of mathematical learning takes place in a child's home (which is probably the most meaningful context for them)? Consider perhaps bath time, setting the table for lunch, completing a jigsaw, and list the mathematical ideas, processes and vocabulary that might be involved in young children's discussions with their families at home. In the case of older children, consider the mathematics that might arise in a discussion on pocket money, times of television programmes, setting the video or preparing a meal.

Merttens (1997) stated that when children learn at home, their learning occurs naturally, as a result of what is happening at the time, and is generally initiated by the child. There is no planned curriculum: children learn about what is real and what fascinates them. Mathematical ideas are nearly always in a real-life context. How is this different from school? Here the teacher plans the curriculum. The teacher guides learning, and generally any questions which are asked come from the teacher. Numbers are almost always represented concretely, with bricks or objects, or abstractly, but these might not be in a real-life context. Can the classroom provide real-life contexts?

These issues highlight what Hughes calls the gap between learning at home and at school which is often manifested in the use of language. Terms such as 'take away', 'table' and 'makes' are used in significantly different ways according to their setting. Hughes, in his book *Children and number* (1986b), suggests that this gap might be closed by teachers by first exploring children's mathematical backgrounds, before planning the curriculum. This would be a form of assessment for learning. Further tasks would then need to be set in meaningful contexts, where children could draw on learning from their homes and lives outside school, allowing them to make human sense of mathematical ideas. Young children should be allowed to use their own invented symbols for number which are valued alongside the conventional symbols. The use of young children's own symbols for mathematics is further explored by Worthington and Carruthers (2003). Older children can also be allowed to describe and evaluate their own methods for calculations. This approach is clearly reflected in the National Numeracy Strategy.

Personal response

Consider your own learning of mathematics, at school, on your ITE course, and in research for lessons you have taught in school. Which tasks have you found easy, and which difficult? In particular, reflect on your learning of more complex mathematical ideas, perhaps at GCSE or A level. Have these tasks been set in a meaningful context, an unmeaning context or in a purely abstract way? Try to relate your memories of learning mathematics to your view of mathematics itself. In your opinion, is mathematics useful? Do you draw on mathematics in your daily life, or is it used most in the classroom or lecture hall?

Is your learning generally more successful in a context where you can see that you will be able to make use of the learning itself at a later date? For example, would it be helpful when you are learning to drive to solve problems to do with speed and acceleration which are not clearly linked to your driving?

Have you ever enjoyed learning mathematics for its own sake, appreciating that although the results of your learning will never be useful in your life, this is an enjoyable and enhancing process?

Contexts for learning

What sort of contexts can be used to enhance children's learning of mathematics? This part of the chapter will study research into the effect contexts have on children's responses to assessment questions.

Evaluate your school's published mathematics scheme or the DfES/QCA Unit Plans, available on **www.standards.dfes.gov.uk**. How are mathematical ideas and questions presented to children? Do contexts, words and illustrations have an impact on children's understanding and confidence to attempt questions set for them? Try also to assess the degree of variety and structure within the examples offered.

Du Feu (2001) argues that some assessment questions and textbooks use real contexts with real problems, naming real people, institutions or products. Further contexts are what he calls 'cleaned'. Here the real context has been simplified in order to suit the need of the task in hand. Other contexts are not real at all, but are contrived to fit a particular objective. They may be inspired by real contexts but the connections have been lost. Some of these he calls 'parables', as they often start as: 'There was once a man with two sons …'. Similarly, he explores the use of names and pictures in mathematical problems. Consider your textbook or unit plan. How are names and pictures used to enhance children's learning, or are they irrelevant?

Other researchers, e.g. Harries and Sutherland (1997), have compared textbooks used internationally and found that the use of pictures, diagrams and contexts differs significantly from country to country.

Blinko (2004) undertook research to explore the effect of contexts on children's achievements in assessment questions. Her research focused on 14 Year 5 children in four different schools. The children were of average ability and were interviewed individually. They were shown a range of assessment questions which involved essentially the same complexity of mathematics in random order. Some were set in realistic contexts, some were bare or decontextualised, and some were in the form of a mathematical puzzle. The children were not given the chance to read the question in great detail but were asked to sort them into three piles: those questions they would have a go at, those they wouldn't, and those they couldn't decide about. The children were much more willing to try questions which were presented with pictures in a realistic context than questions with no context but demanding a similar calculation. On first impressions, questions with pictures were always favoured over those with only words. What are the implications of this research for your own views of mathematics and the way in which you present it to children?

How realistic can contexts set in the classroom be to children, particularly when these are set, as in this case, in an assessment situation? Can realistic situations be created within school? Consider possible activities. If the teacher is to know which contexts do make sense to children, then what does this say about the relationship between teacher and child?

Reflecting on the use of contexts in the classroom

How do contexts affect children's learning? This part of the chapter will reflect in particular on the validity and reliability of assessment tasks set in context. Blinko's research seems to suggest that children prefer assessment questions set in a context, but could the use of a context mislead children? Tasks set in contexts which include unfamiliar words, pictures, or situations with certain conventions and practices could exclude children. This is particularly important when the context is used for assessment purposes. Transfer of existing mathematical learning may not be as easy for all children, who have a variety of backgrounds and life experiences.

The following extract is a transcript of an interviewer discussing the given Standard Assessment Tests question with Mike, an average-ability Year 6 boy.

Extract: Cooper, B (1998) 'Assessing National Curriculum mathematics in England: Exploring children's interpretation of Key Stage 2 tests in clinical interviews'. *Educational Studies in Mathematics*, 35: 38–41.

Organising a competition
David and Gita's group organise a mixed doubles tennis competition. They need to pair a boy with a girl.

They put the three boys' names into one bag and all the three girls' names into another bag.

Find all the possible ways that boys and girls can be paired. Write the pairs below. One pair is already shown.

Rob and Katy

Statement of Attainment 5-6c (from SEAC, 1993).

Mike: Find all the possible ways that the boys and girls can be paired. [pause] There's –
is it – I won't, I won't write it down here, I suppose. Is it because they put their

hand, they go, they put their hand in there first, so they pull out Rob, cos they go right to the bottom first. Then second in the girls they go half way down, so they pick out Katy. Then the boys, they go to the top and pick out David. And they go right to the bottom of the other one to pick out Gita, and you should, you should end up with Rashid and [pause] Ann. [stops]

BC: OK, write those down then.

Mike: Shall I just write who they're going to go with?

BC: Yep.

Mike: Rob and Katy [pause] David and Gita [pause] Rashid and Ann.

BC: Now, before you go on, look at it again. Find all the possible ways that the boys and girls can be paired. All the possible ways. Do you think you've found all the possible ways that boys and girls can be paired?

Mike: There's only one other one. There's only one other way. It's just, just to be lucky who you go with really. That's it just about.

BC: There's only one other way, just to be lucky who you go with?

Mike: Yea, cos they just, they just dip their hand in. They'd probably shake the bag around while they put their hand in, and pick out whoever.

BC: OK, so do you think there are some other ways?

Mike: Only the one I've just said. And that's about it. There's no other possible way unless you took them out – oh, David can go with Gita – and just do that, Rob can go with Ann, and Rashid can go with Katy.

BC: Alright, if you did that though, how many different pairs do you think you could possibly get? If you, if I said, here, write down all the pairs you think you could get, of boys and girls – all the possible ones – do you think there are more than three? Or just three?

Mike: There'd be nine.

BC: There'd be nine? Can you write those nine down, on this page here?

He writes:
David + Ann
Rashid + Katy
Rob + Gita
David + Gita
Rashid + Ann
Rob + Katy
David + Katy
Rashid + Gita
Rob + Ann

BC: Right, how did you know there'd be nine before you started then?

> **Mike:** Because there's three boys and three girls, plus you've got to add another three because – you'll be going David and Ann, Rashid and Katy, Rob and Gita. Put Gita to Ann, Ann to Katy, and Katy to Gita. And then you keep doing that, the same method. So they'd be going, um, from there [pause] from there she'd go to there [he draws linking lines between the names on the diagram of the bag containing girls' names]. She'd go to there, then she'd go to there, then she'd go back up to there, and she'd go down to there, and so on. Nine ti..., three times.
>
> **BC:** Right, so why do you think, when you first did it, you stopped at three then? What was it about the question, do you think?
>
> **Mike:** Um, it [pause] just said, um, find the possible ways, of the boys and girls, were paired. Just says one pair – umm – the way – the way that they're going to be paired, not who they're going to be paired with.

Analysis

How does Mike initially interpret the question? Why do you think this is? Does the context mislead him, or is he initially unable to separate the degree of realism needed to answer the question in the secondary context: that of a question asked in school? If Mike were playing tennis, then it would be of no importance how many pairs are possible. The children would simply need to form pairs and then start the competition. Issues relating to the relative fairness and equality among the pairs would be more important. However, the question, although set in a realistic context, uses the context to present a situation which is in fact unrealistic. Children need to know therefore to what extent they should use their knowledge of the real-life context itself, and to understand the implicit way that questions in school use realistic contexts.

Cooper and Dunne's research (2000) presents evidence that the ability to interpret realistic questions is related to social class and gender.

Children's interpretation of context

The following extract discusses in more detail the relationship between the context in which a question may be set, and the way in which children have to use or disregard their knowledge of the context in real life. These issues will be discussed in more detail in Chapter 6.

Cooper and Harries (2002) 'Children's responses to contrasting 'realistic' mathematics: Just how realistic are children ready to be?' *Educational Studies in Mathematics*, 49, pp1–23.

Steve has bought 4 planks each 2.5 metres long. How many planks 1 metre long can he saw from these planks? (Planks item)

450 soldiers must be bussed to their training site. Each army bus can hold 36 soldiers. How many buses are needed? (Buses item)

John's best time to run 100 metres is 17 seconds. How long will it take him to run 1 kilometre? (Runner item)

Figure 1. Items from Verschaffel *et al.*, 2000, page 19.

There are, of course, at least two competing meanings that might be given to a 'realistic' response to such items. In one sense, a child writing 12.5 for the buses item in Figure 1 might be seen as behaving 'realistically' – or at least fictionally – given that school mathematics problems conventionally have required little attention to the type of realistic considerations that might arise outside of school. However, in the research programme described by Verschaffel *et al.*, a 'realistic' response is taken to mean one which pays some attention to just those sorts of realistic considerations that might characterise problem-solving outside the world of the classroom. From this perspective, in the buses case, a 'realistic' answer would be 13 rather than 12.5. In the case of the planks item in Figure 1 a 'realistic' response would be 8 rather than 10. In the case of the runner item, it clearly is not possible to point to a single correct realistic answer, since a wide range of answers considerably larger than 170 would be sensible responses.

In Verschaffel *et al.*'s (1994) study of 75 10–11-year-old Flemish children's responses to such items, it was found that very few responded 'realistically' in this second sense. While 49% of responses (either the answer itself or a subsequent invited written comment) to the buses item were regarded as 'realistic' in the sense defined by these authors, only 13% of responses to the planks item and just 3% of responses to the runner item were coded as 'realistic'. These findings replicated earlier work by Greer (1993) with 13–14-year-olds in Northern Ireland. Faced with rather stereotypical – and short – word problems, children tend to act without much apparent concern for what would be realistically meaningful outside of the classroom. These authors argue that this is a consequence of the way mathematics is traditionally taught to schoolchildren.

It is possible to raise some critical questions about the way these authors understand certain responses to some of these items as 'realistic' (Cooper and Dunne, 2000a). Ten planks might not be a realistic response to the planks item in the context of building shelving but might be in the context of laying flooring, for example. Neither is it clear that it is always unrealistic to talk about 'twelve and one half' buses. In planning a school trip, we might want 12 and one half buses for the children from one school with three and a half buses for the children then to be picked up from another school, for example. This might total 16 buses but, in everyday speech, we could expect to refer to halves in planning this trip. However, there can be little doubt that the answer of 170 seconds to the runner item in Figure 1 leaves something to be desired from a 'realistic' perspective, especially given the stress in recent years on applicability in mathematics educational circles. Presumably we would prefer children to be able to approach such problems realistically, pointing out that the child would almost certainly slow down after the first one or two hundred metres.

Personal response

What are the implications of this research for test designers and lesson planning?

Consider questions set in your classroom, or in a textbook or unit plan you are familiar with. Are there examples of a confusing use of realistic context?

If so, are there implications for the way in which you teach children to attempt these problems?

If not, then is it possible that the mathematics presented is unconnected to real life?

Analysis

The teaching of problem-solving in mathematics is complex and will be discussed in full in the next chapter. Children need to be exposed to a rich diet of problems and to take time to discuss them in detail. This 'diet' might include real-life problems for which there is no one right answer; puzzles which are valuable in their own right as a means of intriguing children; problems where there is too much information or too little information given; questions which are ambiguous; as well as those which are easily answered. Mathematics is like this in real life.

Your reflections on mathematics in contexts should lead you to consider the relationship between mathematics learnt in school and mathematics in real life. Hughes (1986) and Atkinson (1992) argue that many children see these two as quite separate, even though young children arrive in school with a wealth of mathematical understanding. Mathematics education may reinforce this gap. Is this true of your own teaching of mathematics? If so, it may stem from your own beliefs about mathematics itself. You might believe that mathematics is a fixed and powerful body of knowledge which children need to be initiated into, or you might believe that children need to make their own sense of mathematics, by linking it to their existing knowledge and experiences of the world. Your beliefs in the nature of mathematics are reflected in your relationship with the children you teach, and are indicated by various aspects of teaching and learning in your classroom. For example, your beliefs will be manifested in the types of problems you set for your children, the sort of questions you ask, whether children ask questions of you, whether you make use of your assessments of children's existing knowledge and understanding of mathematics, and their particular life experiences and interests. For further reading on this, see Askew (1997).

Conclusion

Issues surrounding the role of context in supporting children's learning of mathematics have been explored. Contexts clearly can provide a motivation for mathematics, a meaning and a purpose for what can seem to children and adults to be an abstract and sometimes difficult subject. Real-life contexts can provide an opportunity to manipulate and explore mathematical ideas and vocabulary, promoting a fuller understanding. Realistic contexts can be interpreted in various ways, according to the real-life experiences of the learner. Therefore they offer a rich insight into the nature of mathematics itself. Reflection on the complex relationship between context and learning will enhance your understanding of the teaching and learning of mathematics.

6 Problem-solving

By the end of this chapter you should have:

- reflected on **why** it is important to develop children's mathematical problem-solving skills;
- considered **what** benefits may be offered by particular approaches to teaching problem-solving and the issues that are associated with each of them;
- identified **how** your teaching of mathematics may be informed by different perspectives about problem-solving.

Linking your learning

- Mooney, C, Fletcher, M, Briggs, M and McCullouch, J (2002) *Achieving QTS. Primary mathematics: teaching theory and practice* (2nd edition). Exeter: Learning Matters, Chapter 8.
- Mooney, C, Ferrie, L, Fox, S, Hansen, A and Wrathmell, R (2002) *Achieving QTS. Primary mathematics: knowledge and understanding* (2nd edition). Exeter: Learning Matters, Chapter 7.

Professional Standards for QTS
1.7, 2.1, 2.2, 3.3.2

Introduction

The importance of problem-solving within mathematics and the need for children to be taught how to apply their knowledge of mathematics was a key feature of the Cockcroft Report (1982). The Report concluded that: *Mathematics teaching at all levels should include opportunities for … problem solving, including the application of mathematics to everyday situations, and for investigational work* (paragraph 243), and has resulted in these elements of mathematics being given high prominence in the initial and subsequent versions of the National Curriculum for mathematics (DfEE, 1999a). The current version of the National Curriculum indicates that use and application of mathematics should be integrated into all other aspects of the mathematics curriculum, thus reflecting the Cockcroft Report's (1982, p73) assertion that *the ability to solve problems is at the heart of mathematics.*

Different interpretations of the term 'problem-solving' exist and it is important to recognise this. Jones (2003) defines a problem as *an activity where the route to its solution is not immediately obvious.* Such tasks have some degree of openness in that different approaches to solving the problem are possible. If, additionally, a range of solutions is possible then the term 'investigation' is often used instead. The National Curriculum Programme of Study for using and applying mathematics is compatible with this stance. Analysis of the first extract in this chapter (Jones, 1994) will enable us to explore the potential that this type of task offers for developing children's ability to use and apply their mathematical knowledge.

By contrast, the examples in the National Numeracy Strategy (DfEE, 1999b) emphasise the solution of word problems as problem-solving which are 'closed' problems (Jones, 2003), although a careful search will reveal some more open problems. Word problems (such as 'How much change would I receive from a £10 note if I bought items costing £3.20 and £1.99?') are 'closed' tasks in the sense that there is a defined solution and that, once the word problem has been rewritten in a mathematical format using numbers and symbols, there is usually a standard method for performing the resulting calculations. Thus, in terms of the English education system, a continuum of use and application tasks exists with varying degrees of openness (see Figure 6.1).

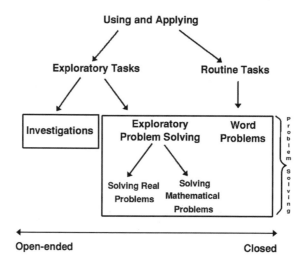

Figure 6.1 Categorising using and applying tasks

Investigations and exploratory problem-solving tasks therefore offer children greater opportunities for developing higher-order mathematical thinking skills. In the second extract in this chapter Askew (2003) argues, however, that word problems can still offer valuable opportunities for developing children's mathematical thinking.

Traditionally in the UK problems have been treated as contexts in which children can apply existing knowledge. This is reflected in the use of the term 'using and applying mathematics' within the National Curriculum (DfEE, 1999a). In the Netherlands, problem-solving is viewed somewhat differently. Problem-solving contexts are used as a starting point from which mathematical conceptual understanding and strategies are developed. The final extract in this chapter (van den Heuvel-Panhuizen, 2002) examines the rationale that underlies this approach to teaching problem-solving, known as 'realistic mathematics education'.

Personal response

- What do you consider to be mathematical problem-solving?
- In what contexts do you use mathematics to solve problems in everyday life?
- What mathematical skills do you use in solving these types of problems?

Exploratory problem-solving

As preparation for reading the following extract, you should read:

- Hughes, M, Desforges, C and Mitchell, C (1999) *Numeracy and beyond: Applying mathematics in the primary school* (available at **www.standards.dfes. gov.uk/primary/profdev/mathematics/raisingstandardsks1/** Guide for your professional development, Book 4, Appendix 2).

Extract: Jones, L (1994) 'Reasoning, logic and proof at Key Stage 2'. *Mathematics in School,* **November: 6–8.**

I asked each of the children to give me a small number, less than 10. For each number I wrote down the number, and two consecutive numbers.

4, 5, 6

2, 3, 4

7, 8, 9

I asked the children to find the total of each row, then asked them to comment on anything they noticed. They discussed which 'times tables' they appeared in; 'the 2 times, the 5 times and the 9 times'.

LJ: 'Do they all come into one of the tables?' (A leading question!)
        'Yes, they are all in the 3 times.'

They tried some more examples to see if the total was always a multiple of 3. For each example they worked out how many threes gave the total and wrote this alongside:

4, 5, 6 3×5

2, 3, 4 3×3

7, 8, 9 3×8

5, 6, 7 3×6

LJ: 'They are all in the three times table. Why is that then?'
Nikki: 'I think it's because they're all next to each other. 'Cos they're next to each other they come in the three times table.'
This statement was one of those which leave you wondering whether it was a 'shot in the dark', an amazing piece of insight or simply the child bringing together the significant pieces of information about the numbers we were considering.

I tried to explore this idea further by setting out groups of counters to represent the numbers we were considering.
Nikki: 'They're all 3 numbers so they must be in the 3 times table.'

LJ: 'Nikki, I can see you have got an idea. Can you try to explain again?'

Nikki: 'There are 3 numbers; 1, 2, 3; 4, 5, 6; 7, 8, 9. Is it because of the three numbers? Is it because they're next to each other?'

LJ: 'We know that 3, 4, 5 makes the same as 3 × 4. Can you use the counters to show me that?'

'Take away one from the three and add it to the four and that makes 5. Then add the five and the five together and then add the two and that makes an even number that is in an odd and even times table.'

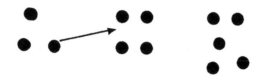

It is interesting that this method relies on the construction of 12 in its most familiar form i.e. as 5 + 5 + 2, rather than shifting directly from 3, 4, 5 to 3 × 4. The child has focused on the number 12, rather than the sets of 4.

I tried again, laying out piles of 4, 5 and 6 counters.

'How can we make that into 3 fives?'

Nikki moved a counter from the pile of 6 to the pile of 4.

'I took one away from the four [sic], so that's 5. Put it here so that's a 5 and then that's a 5.

LJ: 'Let's try it with a different number.'

Nikki: 'You could probably do it with any number.'

Helen: 'You could probably do it with any number. It could be because there's an even in it.'

Helena and Nikki had the counters and were talking through the moves.

Nikki was able to demonstrate how you could make three equal piles from any three consecutive numbers. I offered her large numbers to think about and she could describe how they could be shown to be multiples of three. During this session Nikki developed a very clear idea of this number pattern, supported by visual images of the numbers. She was able to demonstrate a way of proving that this pattern would hold for a general case. The language she used for this; 'You could probably do it with any number,' is tentative, but she was well on the way to personal confidence in the stability of this conjecture.

Analysis

This task is not drawn from a 'real life' context, unlike those discussed in the article by Hughes *et al.* (2000). However, it does have intrinsic mathematical value because the sums of sets of three consecutive numbers provide a pattern which is mathematically interesting to explore, and this is demonstrated in the extract by the children's engagement with the task. We can conclude that both real-life and purely mathematical problems have value in offering opportunities to develop children's ability to use and apply mathematical knowledge and understanding.

Hughes *et al.* (2000) noted that in using and applying activities the teacher has the constant dilemma of deciding when and how to intervene. While it is important that the teacher allows children sufficient freedom to enable them to select their own strategies and approaches and to make their own decisions during the process of solving a problem or tackling an investigation, the teacher may also wish to intervene strategically by modelling strategies explicitly or by asking questions which lead children to engage in higher levels of mathematical thinking. Such questions or prompts should cause children to think more deeply (e.g. about being systematic, at higher levels of abstraction or in more divergent, creative fashion) but should, as far as possible, avoid prescribing what children should do or think thereafter.

Of course, the above is an ideal which is not always attainable. For example, young children or children who are unaccustomed to exploratory forms of mathematical activity are more likely to need greater direction from the teacher when beginning to delve into a problem or investigation before they can make progress. They are also likely to need further intervention from the teacher as the activity continues. In a similar vein, the teacher will also need to intervene more prescriptively should children become so 'stuck' that high levels of frustration are becoming evident, but even in such circumstances it is possible to phrase this guidance in an open-ended manner. Questions such as 'Have you thought about trying …?', 'Do you think this might work?' or 'Would it help to … ?' can offer children possible directions to consider.

In the extract above, Jones' role is critical in supporting the development of the children's reasoning skills. Consider the questions and interventions by Jones in the extract. The initial request allows children freedom to explore the context using the strategies that they have at their disposal. Jones encourages the children to search for, or to explain, patterns and relationships, thus promoting awareness of the mathematics inherent in this context. However, the range of answers which ensues indicates that the children are beginning to flounder aimlessly. Therefore, Jones asks a (self-acknowledged) 'leading question' in order to offer more structure and direction to the children's thinking. This then enables the children to continue their exploration further by considering more sets of consecutive numbers.

The next intervention by Jones encourages the children to explain the pattern they have discovered, thus requiring the children to articulate their thinking about their understanding of the mathematical relationships involved. Jones' suggestion that the children should use the counters to show that $3 + 4 + 5 = 3 \times 4$ is a further attempt to help the children to clarify their thinking in the hope that they may adopt a strategy of rearranging the counters to establish this. However, the children's initial rearrangement of the counters is unhelpful in this respect, so Jones offers a different set of three consecutive numbers and asks: *How can we make that into 3 fives?* This is sufficient for Nikki to produce a different rearrangement, which enables her to develop towards a generalised line of reasoning that applies to any three consecutive numbers (i.e. that subtracting one from the highest of the three consecutive numbers and adding it to the lowest will produce three amounts, each equal to the middle number). While this is not a formal mathematical proof, it enables Nikki to reach a personal certainty about her conjecture regarding the sums of three consecutive numbers and indicates an ability to form conjectures from the exploration of a few cases and to establish or refute the wider applicability of such conjectures to all possible cases by the use of reasoning, a key aim of use and application tasks. However, what is less certain is whether Nikki will be able to transfer the understanding, strategies and skills acquired in this context to other contexts in the future. As Gravemeijer (1997, pp343–5) states, generalising by recognising connections between contexts which have been explored is not the same as transfer from an explored context to one which has yet to be explored.

The extract indicates that a delicate balance is required between sensitive questioning which develops the children's thinking, and allowing children time and some degree of freedom to develop their own approaches and strategies. In this sense, the teacher's role is somewhat different from that when teaching other aspects of the mathematics curriculum. Hughes *et al.* (2000) conclude that understanding of the likely consequences of intervention and non-intervention and flexibility of approach by the teacher are critical in such contexts.

Personal response

- What aspects of problem-solving are important to teach?
- How can you ensure that your teaching allows children appropriate degrees of freedom to explore problems?
- What are the implications for your planning of 'using and applying' activities?

In the light of your responses to these:

- Identify the problem-solving skills used by the children in the extract and compare these with the requirements of the National Curriculum for teaching children about using and applying mathematics.
- Locate the pages of examples in the National Numeracy Strategy entitled 'Reasoning about numbers and shapes'. Discuss with your peers how you might use these types of task to develop children's ability to investigate general statements and to make their own generalisations.
- Try teaching some exploratory problem-solving activities in the classroom. Then reflect on whether your decisions about when and how to intervene were appropriate.

Word problems

Before reading the following extract, read Askew, M and Wiliam, D (1995) *Recent research in mathematics education 5–16*. London: HMSO, pp22–3 (available at **www.standards.dfes.gov.uk/primary/profdev/mathematics/raisingstandardsks2/** Guide for your professional development, Book 3, Appendix 3).

In the extract, Askew draws on Treffers' (1991) notions of 'vertical' and 'horizontal' mathematising in order to explore some of the complexities of two word problems attempted by a Year 3 class. The children tried to use trial-and-improvement strategies but struggled with a first problem: 'Mrs Chang bought some video tapes. She bought five tapes each costing the same amount. She spent £35. How much did each tape cost?' However, the children were able to use finger-counting strategies to successfully solve an apparently similar, second problem: 'Mr Chang bought some video tapes. He bought some tapes costing £7 each. He spent £42. How many tapes did he buy?'

Extract: Askew, M (2003) 'Word problems: Cinderellas or wicked witches?', in Thompson, I (ed) *Enhancing primary mathematics teaching*. Maidenhead: Open University Press.

When acting in the real world, some 'problems' are solved by direct action: I want a nail in the wall, I hammer it in. But problems in classrooms, and particularly word problems, usually require setting up some representation or model to 'act' upon, rather than act on the actual situation. The children discussed above did not go and get real video tapes to help them, they used their fingers to represent the tapes. Fingers are still part of the real world but not part of the world of video tapes. So in the course of setting up this representation, the children have engaged in the act of mathematising the situation. And this is a horizontal mathematising: a move from 'the perceived objects to the world of symbols' (Treffers 1991: 32). Even though fingers can still be perceived they have not been used as fingers *per se* but as a representation of something else. A model has been set up and horizontal mathematising has taken place.

But setting up a model in this way is not the end of the story. The model itself may have to be adapted and changed: shifts may be made in the world of representations and symbols. Such shifts would involve vertical mathematising.

Horizontal mathematising
An analysis of the mathematical reasonings involved in the Mr and Mrs Chang problems illustrates the complementary processes of horizontal and vertical mathematising. Through analysing in detail the processes involved in these two problems, I hope to show why solving either of them is a much more complicated process than it might first appear to be.

Taking Mr Chang's problem first, stripping the essence of the problem out of the context leads to 'reading' the problem as 'what do I have to multiply 7 by to get 42?' This can be expressed as an initial mathematical model:

$$7 \times \square = 42$$

This is the mathematical model that the children implicitly worked with when counting on in sevens to 42. And it is one that they found easy to work with. (Note that here, and in what follows, I am interpreting $7 \times \square$ as '7 multiplied by something' not '7 times something'. The children, in counting on in sevens with their fingers, were figuring out what to multiply seven by, or times it by.)

Turning to Mrs Chang, the essence of her problem is 'what number do I have to multiply 5 by to get 35?' Symbolically:

$\square \times 5 = 35$

This is more difficult to represent in the physical world – you have to guess at what goes in the box and hence the children's difficulty with this problem.

Vertical mathematising

Although the children set up representations of the problem through horizontal mathematising, none of them went on further to recast the model through vertical mathematising (i.e. working with the symbols). Further analysis shows why this is a far from straightforward process.

In the Mr Chang problem, where an initial mathematical model of $7 \times \square = 42$ was set up, we can use the fact that division is the inverse of multiplication to set up the mathematically equivalent model $42 \div \square = 7$. Now this mathematical model is not the easiest to solve. As adults we 'know' that an equivalent equation is $42 \div 7 = \square$. But note that this is only equivalent mathematically. If we perform horizontal mathematising in the reverse direction, from the mathematical world to the real world, $42 \div \square = 7$ and $42 \div 7 = \square$ do not lead to the same situation. 'What do we have to divide 42 by to get 7' ($42 \div \square = 7$) is a question that arises from very different situations from those that give rise to 'what do we get when 42 is divided by 7?' ($42 \div 7 = \square$). Compare 'I want to put 42 apples equally into seven bags, how many do I have to put into each bag?' with 'I want to put 42 apples into bags, with seven in each bag'.

Strictly speaking, to get from $42 \div \square = 7$ to $42 \div 7 = \square$ there is an intermediate (and largely implicit) step in the vertical mathematising process:

$7 \times \square = 42$

$\square \times 7 = 42$

$\square = 42 \div 7$

Since most adults just 'know' that seven sixes are 42 these vertical mathematising shifts are usually not necessary (or at least not done consciously) and this level of analysis may have the feel of a sledgehammer to crack a nut. But both the need for and the power of this vertical mathematising become clearer if we make the numbers less familiar. Suppose Mr Chang is a wholesaler who buys some stereos at £78 each and spends a total of £1404. Which would you solve

$78 \times \square = 1404$ or $1404 \div 78 = \square$?

The latter is more straightforward to calculate, but, as pointed out above, does not actually 'mirror' the action of the real-world situation. Mathematical equivalence does not correspond with real-world equivalence.

Perversely, the vertical mathematising steps in the Mrs Chang problem are more straightforward. Because multiplication is commutative, $\square \times 5 = 35$ can be vertically mathematised in one step to:

$5 \times \square = 35$

But notice that the children did not do this. Instead they took guesses at what might go in the box (I am not suggesting of course that they were aware of doing this). Although they might 'know' that $\square \times 5 = 5 \times \square$, when it comes to 'uncoupling' from the real-world context and moving around the mathematical world instead, children find this difficult.

Analysis

The extract indicates some of the complexities of solving word problems. Consider the children's use of models (in this case, fingers) as a way of mathematising the Mr Chang problem. The use of the model supports the children's thinking within the purely mathematical context and enables them to achieve an answer by trial-and-improvement techniques. This corresponds closely to research findings which show that children make use of a wide range of informal strategies to solve word problems (De Corte and Verschaffel, 1987). However, mere use of an appropriate model is not sufficient for many children to solve a word problem. It is quite common for children to struggle with word problems even if they are able to perform the equivalent number calculation when devoid of context. Word problems require children to translate between the real world context and the world of mathematics and back again (see Figure 6.2).

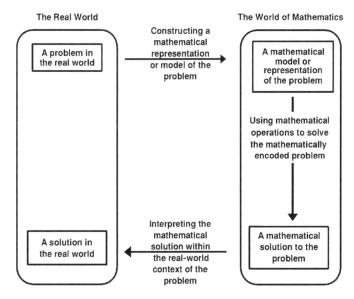

Figure 6.2 Solving a word problem

Askew (2003) indicates that there are considerable difficulties for children in 'uncoupling' the mathematics from the context of the problem in order to undertake subtle vertical mathematisations because of the mismatch between the physical world and the mathematical world. The context of the problem determines which models (physical or mental) children may adopt to represent this. However, the selection of a strategy for performing the resulting calculation is best determined by considering the numbers involved rather than the context, and the most efficient calculation strategy may well not make sense in relation to the original context. This would appear to be a substantial obstacle to success given that children's informal strategies for solving a word problem reflect closely the semantic structure of the problem (De Corte and Verschaffel, 1987).

However, awareness of this issue on the part of the teacher may provide a way forward. Askew (2003) criticises the common approach of treating each word problem as a separate entity and superficial strategies such as teaching children to locate key words within them in order to ascertain the meaning because the key words will indicate 'actions' which are context-dependent and this may *restrict children's ability to do vertical mathematisation* (Askew, 2003, p83). He suggests that children could be asked to compare problems (such as the two in the extract) in order to help them appreciate more deeply the complexities of solving such problems.

In a similar vein, Askew also advocates helping children to categorise word problems in order to help them appreciate structural similarities and differences. Categorising problems will require children to use reasoning skills in order to make generalisations about solution strategies for particular classes of problems. For example, Riley *et al.* (1983) classified one-step addition and subtraction problems into three categories: change, combine and compare problems. Each of these categories can be subdivided further according to the position of the unknown quantity (initial, second or final). Research indicates that children find change problems and combine problems easier to solve than comparison problems, and problems with an unknown final quantity are much easier than those with an unknown initial quantity (Verschaffel and De Corte, 1997).

Personal response

- To what extent do word problems provide realistic contexts for problem-solving?
- Reflect on whether the progression adopted by the National Numeracy Strategy examples (one-step, two-step, multi-step) acknowledges the issues raised in the analysis above.
- How could you adapt the National Numeracy Strategy progression (where appropriate) in order to help children develop strategies for solving word problems?
- What teaching strategies will you use to promote successful word problem-solving?

- Locate some of the one-step addition and subtraction word problems in the National Numeracy Strategy (DfEE, 1999) and categorise them as either change, combine or compare problems. Then analyse them for their potential for vertical and horizontal mathematisation.

- Analyse some school textbooks in order to consider to what degree the progression offered for solving word problems acknowledges the issues raised above.

Realistic mathematics education

In the Netherlands a different attitude to problem-solving has been adopted. This approach, known as realistic mathematics education (RME), is based upon Freudenthal's (1968) belief that children should be given 'guided' opportunities to 're-invent' mathematics through doing it. Thus, the focus of RME is children's mathematisation of contexts which are meaningful to them (the term 'realistic' is derived from the Dutch *zich realiseren*, meaning 'to imagine') and through this participation in the learning process children develop mathematical understanding and strategies. Treffers' (1978, 1987) perception of two types of mathematisation (horizontal and vertical – encountered earlier in the discussion of the Askew article) has been used as a means of describing different types of learning within this process of mathematisation. Instead of using problem-solving as a vehicle for context-based application of earlier learning as is traditional in England, RME uses context problems as a source for the learning process.

Before you read the extract that follows, you may wish to read Treffers, A and Beishuizen, M (1999) 'Realistic mathematics education in the Netherlands', in Thompson, I (ed) *Issues in teaching numeracy in primary schools*. Buckingham: Open University Press.

Extract: van den Heuvel-Panhuizen, M (2002) 'Realistic mathematics education as work in progress', in F L Lin (ed) *Common sense in mathematics education*, Proceedings of 2001 The Netherlands and Taiwan Conference on Mathematics Education, 19–23 November 2001, Taipei, Taiwan: National Taiwan Normal University.

The following example demonstrates even more strongly the role of the context in building up mathematical knowledge. This example involves the context of a city bus.[5] The bus problem that is based on this context turned out to be a very powerful learning environment for first graders. First of all, this problem offers students opportunities to develop a formal mathematical language. The teaching starts with a 'real life' situation in which the students have to act as the driver of a city bus. The passengers are getting on and off the bus, and at each stop the students have to determine the number of passengers in the bus. Later the same is done on paper (see the worksheet in Figure 6).

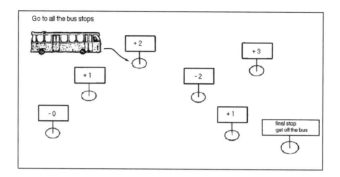

Figure 6 Bus problem[6]

The development of mathematical language is elicited by the need to keep track of what happened during the ride of the bus. Initially the language is closely connected to the context, but later on it is also used for describing other situations. Gradually, the bus context loses its narrative feature and takes on more of a model character. The following student work (see Figure 7) reflects how the context-connected mathematical language can evolve progressively to a more general formal mathematical language.

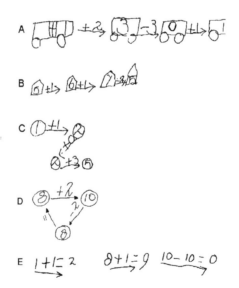

Figure 7 Student work bus problem[7]

What started as a context-connected report of the story of the bus (A), is later used for numerical operations in other contexts, e.g. keeping track of the number of customers that are in a shop (B), and for expressing operations with pure numbers (C and D).[8] In (E) the transition to the standard way of notating number sentences is visible.

In addition to offering the students a learning environment for developing a formal mathematical language that makes sense to them, the bus context – and particularly the context of the bus stop – is also very suitable to elicit mathematical reasoning. Evidence for this suitability was illuminated by developmental research on negative numbers carried out by Streefland (1996). In a Dutch grade five-six classroom he presented the students – who never had dealt with negative number before – the problem that is pictured in Figure 8 and asked them first how many passengers were in the bus after the bus left the bus stop. Then he asked them the challenging question of what else could have happened at the bus stop with the same result in terms of passengers in the bus after the bus stop. Figure 9 shows how the students worked out this question.

in   out

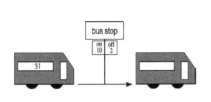

Figure 8 Getting on and off the bus   Figure 9 Bus stop stories

Later on in the lesson, the students could even use the bus stop model to generate problems with a fixed starting number and a fixed result (see Figure 10).

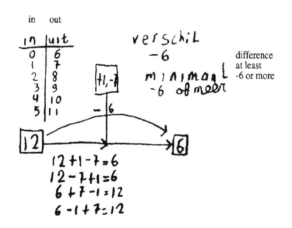

Figure 10 Student-generated problems based on experiences with the bus stop context

The bus and the bus stop context are an example of how experiences from a 'daily life' situation can be the impetus for growth in mathematical understanding. Compared to the context of the stickers this bus context evolves to a model to support mathematical thinking. An important requirement for models functioning in this way is that they are rooted in concrete situations and that they are also flexible enough to be useful in higher levels of mathematical activities. This means that the models will provide the students with a foothold during the process of vertical mathematisation, without obstructing the path back to the source.

Connected models as the backbone of progress

As became already visible in the previous examples, progress implies that students arrive at more general solutions from context-related solutions. Contexts that have model potential serve as an important device for bridging this gap between informal and more formal mathematics. First, the students develop strategies closely connected to the context. Later on, certain aspects of the context situation can become more general, which means that the context more or less acquires the character of a model and as such can give support for solving other, but related, problems. Eventually, the models give the students access to more formal mathematical knowledge.

In order to make the shift from the informal to the formal level possible, the models have to modify from a 'model of' a particular situation (e.g. a scheme that represents the situation of passengers getting on and off the bus at a bus stop) to a 'model for' all kinds of other, but equivalent, situations (e.g. a scheme that can be used for expressing shop attendance, but that also can be used to find number pairs that give the same increase or decrease as a result).[9]

This important role of models has all to do with the level principle of RME. This principle implies that learning mathematics is considered as passing through various levels of understanding: from the ability to invent informal context-related solutions, to the creation of various levels of shortcuts and schematisations, to the acquisition of insight into the underlying principles and the discernment of even broader relationships. Crucial for arriving at the next level is the ability to reflect on the activities conducted before.[10]

5   The use of this context was an idea of Van den Brink.
6   Picture is an adapted version from Van den Brink (1989).
7   Picture is taken from Van den Brink (1989).
8   Although in (C) pure numbers are used, the shape of the notation betrays that it still represents an operation with context numbers.
9   For more about the idea of 'model of' and 'model for' see Section 2 of this paper and Note 1.
10 This idea of accumulated reflection was based on the work of the Van Hieles (see Freudenthal, 1991).

Analysis

The extract indicates clearly the RME principle of developing children's conceptual understanding and related strategies from within the contexts of problems. The 'bus ride' example in the extract illustrates neatly how the progression in learning is structured and developed. By working within the contexts of problems, children acquire mathematical understanding of context-related strategies, thus mathematising horizontally. Later, vertical mathematisation occurs as the initial strategies which are derived from within the contexts are refined to become more efficient and more widely applicable. Similarly, as aspects of the contexts are gradually generalised, 'emergent' mathematical models (Gravemeijer, 2001, p156) of the contexts are then transformed into models for other, equivalent situations. Further horizontal mathematisation then becomes possible as the more generalised strategies and models are applied to other equivalent or related contexts. Differentiation is facilitated by allowing children to respond to problems at their own level of understanding, thus enabling the use of inter-active whole-class teaching and reflection. Identifying problem contexts which possess the potential for developing 'models of' the context into 'models for' other kinds of situations (Streefland, 1985, 1991) is, therefore, crucial in the teaching progression in RME. Also significant is the recognition that those models which provide longitudinal coherence through the connections they provide between different contexts are the most powerful in supporting children's progress (van den Heuvel-Panhuizen, 2002).

Personal response

- How is the RME approach similar to, and different from, the UK approach to problem-solving?
- Reflect on the role of the teacher in the RME approach to mathematics.
- What aspects of RME might be used within a series of UK mathematics lessons? What would be the advantages and disadvantages of doing so?
- Read about other RME problem-solving contexts using the Reference list.
- Try using an RME-style problem as a starting point for children to learn some mathematics. Evaluate the advantages and disadvantages of this approach to teaching and learning mathematics.
- Consider which, if any, of the example problems listed in the National Numeracy Strategy could provide the starting point for an RME approach.

Conclusion

A consideration of some different approaches to teaching problem-solving will inevita-bly lead to a consideration of the purpose of teaching problem-solving. In the UK, the aims have been twofold: preparation for everyday life through applying existing knowl-edge to other situations and the development of higher-level mathematical skills such as generalising. Nickson (2000, p177) asserts that:

> a problem-solving approach has clear benefits for pupils in helping them to ap-proach mathematical problems of all kinds in a more structured way. Practice in identifying the main features of a problem and rejecting redundant information, and looking for relationships and strategies in a problem-solving situation, are all transferable skills that can be used in all areas of mathematics.

However, Askew and Wiliam (1995, pp26–7) and Hughes *et al.* (2000, p6) indicate that such transferability of skills, knowledge and understanding is not trivial. A key chal-lenge, therefore, is to determine how best to ensure that children learn mathematics in ways that enable them to transfer knowledge and understanding gained in one context to other contexts they encounter subsequently.

In the Netherlands, relevance to everyday life is ensured by using everyday contexts (and strategies related to those contexts) as a starting point for learning rather than as an end point for application. In this sense, the UK approach has been the reverse of that in the Netherlands. Moreover, there is a greater sense of progression and continuity between problem contexts in the Netherlands through the use of models which are developed through a continuous process of evaluation and research. In contrast, the progression for problem-solving offered in the National Numeracy Strategy appears somewhat simplistic and limited in breadth. In both countries, however, the role of the teacher is regarded as important in supporting children's learning through problem-solving.

7 Making decisions about mathematics and ICT

By the end of this chapter you should have:

- reflected on **why** you use ICT within your mathematics lessons;
- considered **what** ICT you use in your mathematics teaching;
- identified **how** ICT can be best used to secure effective learning and teaching.

Linking your learning

- DfEE (1999) *The National Numeracy Strategy.* London: DfEE Publications, Introduction.
- Mooney, C, Fletcher, M, Briggs, M and McCullouch, J (2002) *Achieving QTS. Primary mathematics: teaching theory and practice* (2nd edition). Exeter: Learning Matters, Chapters 2, 10 and 11.

Professional Standards for QTS
2.5, 3.3

Introduction

The use of ICT and its inclusion within the teaching and learning process ought to be a non-negotiable part of classroom practice. Many would not necessarily agree, but this does not mean that ICT has to be an omnipresent feature of each and every mathematics lesson. The principles enshrined with the National Numeracy Strategy (DfEE, 1999, p32) should prevail:

> You should use computer software in your daily maths lesson only if it is the most efficient and effective way to meet your lesson's objectives.

Professional judgement is the crucial factor, and it is this element that this chapter concerns itself with.

From the outset it is important to clarify what is meant by ICT. In recent years there has been a concentration within schools upon technology development that is computer based; a result of the government pupil/PC target ratio of 1:8 by August 2004 outlined within the National Grid for Learning (NGfL) initiative (1999). However, this is a rather limited view of what constitutes ICT. Sharp *et al.* (2000) and Smith (1999), for example, clearly indicate the variety of technology available for teachers to use within the classroom. This includes:

- computers, with a range of software;
- digital camera;
- video camera;
- interactive whiteboard;

- calculator;
- audio cassette recorder;
- video cassette recorder;
- the internet;
- programmable floor robots;
- television;
- overhead projectors (OHPs);
- OHP calculator.

It is the whole of this range that should be drawn upon, where appropriate, to develop and extend children's mathematical learning.

There are several factors that influence teachers' decisions about using ICT. Perceived government pressure is one. ITT Standard S2.5 (TTA, 2002) focuses on the need to demonstrate the appropriate use and inclusion of ICT within the classroom. Newly qualified teachers are required to pass the ICT skills test as a condition of achieving QTS status. Since 1999, successive governments have invested millions of pounds through ring-fenced NGfL funding for ICT infrastructure and training and New Opportunities Fund (NOF) funding for skills training. As a result there has been an underlying message highlighting the importance and significance of using ICT within the classroom. This, it can be argued with some conviction, has resulted in teachers feeling pressured to include ICT within their mathematics lessons.

Enthusiastic colleagues are another influencing factor in the school context (Cox, 1997). They frequently and earnestly extol the virtues of a particular programme or 'share' how ICT helped a child to grasp a particular idea, and can have an impact in influencing practice. We can often be inspired to respond by trying these ideas out in our own classrooms as a result of this modelling of school practice.

Various perceived obligations are identified by Fox *et al.* (2000) that add to these influences. Technological advances and market pressure accompany expectation, linked to government expectation, to generate an additional influence within classroom practice. Added to these promptings, there are also reports (OFSTED, 2002) that indicate that teachers believe that using ICT is a significant feature in improving teaching and learning within the classroom. Are all these reasons valid, or should there be a higher imperative for including ICT?

Making decisions

What ICT will you use and why?

With these issues in mind, read the following.

Extract: Perks, P (2002) 'The interactive whiteboard: Implications for software and design'. *BSRLM*, 22(1) pp55–59.

Utilitarian or pedagogical?
Software designed or used for educational purposes can be designated in two ways, according to its usefulness (utilitarian) or ways it may transform teaching (pedagogical).

In business, the decisions are utilitarian. In teaching the pedagogical are considered obvious. I wish to argue that both the utilitarian and pedagogical aspects of software need to be more explicit for mathematics teaching.

Pedagogy needs to be considered in both the design of software and in its use. Of course, there is not just one style of teaching with software. One useful way of considering the pedagogical aspects of ICT is described by Hewitt (2001) as that which works on assisting memory and that which educates awareness.

Senior management may concentrate on the utilitarian values of using ICT. Oldknow and Taylor (2000) suggest for the school ICT may 'improve efficiency and reduce teaching costs' (p. 226). For teachers, utilitarian uses might be improving efficiency and reducing the burden of administration. For pedagogy, ICT may 'be a stimulus to re-thinking their approach to mathematics teaching' or 'be a stimulus to re-thinking their understanding of mathematics' (p. 225). The utilitarian aspects may initially be the more important way to encourage teachers to use software in their teaching, but it is the pedagogical that may be more important for design to enhance teaching.

Large enough to see

If you want to use one computer as a basis for work with the whole class, any work needs to be seen. The discovery that Excel allowed font sizes so large that a single number could fill the monitor and be generated randomly allowed me to design my own files. My first whole class use was with a file that generated random numbers to be used as bearings. The class task was based on students pointing in the direction of the bearing. The numbers were in multiples of 10, from 0 to 350. On a PC, pressing F9 recalculates the Excel workbook and produces a new number according to the formula. Analysis can be according to utilitarian and pedagogical characteristics.

Utilitarian	**Pedagogical**
Large font	Whole class involvement possible
Numbers can be generated as many times as possible	Opportunities for practice can be extended
Machine chooses the numbers according to a formula	The teaching decision – e.g. the use of multiples of 10 is made explicit by the choice of formula
The computer chooses the numbers and the order of presentation	There is an apparent shift in the perception of the task by students. The computer is seen as independent whereas many assume that the teacher is manipulating the choice in an undeclared manner
The computer stores the file ready for the next time (not as easily lost as as flash cards)	More, similar practice becomes possible because the tools are available
The formula can be quickly adapted	The task can be changed to suit other mathematical content

My initial changes to the formula were for use when practising angle, limiting the higher number to 90, 180 or 380 depending on whether the students were working on acute angles or extending to obtuse and reflex angles. Although these were pedagogical decisions, the task remains within the aspect of assisting memory. There seems no obvious way to extend use to the education of awareness.

As a teacher I like to use my materials for as many situations as possible. So I began to think of activities for which I used numerical flash cards, such as chanting tables, e.g. see a number ending in 6 and subtract 7 from it. This lead to an extension of the file that allowed a new set of numbers simply by typing them into cells.

The pedagogical implications of choosing the set of numbers was highlighted when a primary teacher using the file comments that she used numbers from 0.25 with a gap of 0.25 for doubling then doubling. As her children worked on chanting responses, they realised that they always got whole numbers. Her pedagogical intention was to connect the 'fourness' of 'double, double' with the quarters hidden in the decimal numbers, the practice (assisting memory) was now enabling some children to work on the relationships between the different structures of number (educating awareness).

The design of the file had been utilitarian; it suited me to be able to change the set of numbers quickly. The implications of the design change were, however, pedagogical. The earlier example, subtracting seven from numbers of the form 10n+6, initially focused on practice, but allows a chance to work on structure. This adaptability allows the file to become a more powerful tool for the classroom. What is important to stress is that many of the files do not, in themselves, permit the education of awareness, it is the pedagogical decisions, the teacher choices, which allow them to become useful and interesting tools for learning mathematics.

The interactive electronic whiteboard
But two aspects of the IWB are worth considering separately; the ability to write on the software and save this and any other images and the style of 'interactivity' the IWB allows.

Writing and saving
The 'saving' aspect of the IWB offers similar advantages to those above, the extra facility is that anything is saved in the moment. Spontaneous teaching/learning situations can be captured. The IWB offers a powerful new feature; anything written or 'snapped' in the lesson can be revisited.

Utilitarian	**Pedagogical**
Allows notes to be saved	The learner can ask to revisit any aspect of the lesson, examples are always available
You can write on top of a software application	Conjectures can be compared with or tested against the software
You can write in different colours and/ or on top of different copies of the same software	Difference approaches can be recorded and contrasted at other times
	The relative merits of different conjectures can be discussed
	Errors can be worked on collaboratively

Interactivity

The whiteboard allows access to any of the menus or buttons via contact with the board. Handwriting recognition or the on-screen keyboard permit other aspects of programs to be controlled. Interaction with the software is not tied to the keyboard, but is related more to the traditional pointing at the board, familiar to teachers over the years. Standing close to the images, pointing at, directing changes, all of these add to a very different feel, a closer sense of working with the ICT.

Analysis

This article highlights two significant reasons why ICT should be employed in mathematics teaching:

- as a tool to assist the delivery of the session;
- as a resource to secure the development of mathematical skills and understanding of the mathematical ideas being considered.

It is important that there is clarity in the decision-making process. Firstly, there must be recognition that there is a decision to be made. There should be no automatic exclusion, even though ICT Luddites are thought to be a 'dying breed' (Poulter and Basford, 2003, p4). Neither should there be automatic inclusion of ICT as a response to the aforementioned pressures. Rather, a professional consideration of the resources available and the mathematics being taught should result in a clear decision about whether ICT should be included and what it should be.

For example, in the circumstances described in the extract, it would be appropriate to use PowerPoint to generate a sequence of numbered cards where children consider the probability of the next card being higher or lower than the one on display. This use of ICT enables the teacher's delivery of the session to be more effective. Another example would be to use an interactive whiteboard to demonstrate rotational symmetry of an equilateral triangle. This helps children to visualise this mathematical idea.

When making the decision about whether to use ICT, there are other considerations to be aware of. For example, considering the interactive whiteboard, Knight et al. (2004) identified five contexts in which this technology can be utilised: teacher as demonstrator; teacher as modeller; teacher in control – inviting the children to discuss the mathematics, where it is shared; children in control, with the 'teacher' advising or guiding them; and children working independently. Being able to identify specific contexts in which ICT plays a particular role supports the decision-making process (see Chapter 5).

Being aware of research that supports effective teaching and learning also plays a part in this decision-making process. The King's College research (Askew et al., 1997) on effective teachers of numeracy suggests that the most effective mathematics teachers are 'connectionists'. These teachers linked different areas of mathematics. For example, by using floor turtles, children are encouraged to make connections with their understanding of angle and direction within a problem-solving context.

Personal response

Other practical considerations require thought. Fox *et al.* (2000) identify time pressures and resource issues that will impact upon our decisions. Questions to consider here include: What do I want the ICT to do? Is there a place for programmes that provide drill and practice opportunities? What about integrated learning systems? Can these fit with current classroom practice? In responding to these issues, much will depend upon teachers' attitudes and beliefs about mathematics, what constitutes good practice and how ICT can support learning.

How ICT can develop children's learning – the communication principle

When there is only one computer in the classroom, a well-used organisational strategy is to run paired or small-group work at the computer. It has been suggested by Fox *et al.* (2000) that one reason for adopting this strategy has been the benefits that it offers in enabling collaborative working and the development of children's linguistic interaction. However, there is also recognition that this view might be simplistic, with an awareness of research by Mercer and Wegerif (1998) that indicates the prevalence of pressures related to equality of provision for a class of children within a limited time frame. Nevertheless, 'pupil talk' must be considered as a valid by-product of the children's work at the computer. But we must also consider to what extent this happens. It is not enough to plan for the vague hope of language development as a result of using ICT.

Extract: Monaghan, F (2004) 'Thinking together – Using ICT to develop collaborative thinking and talk in mathematics'. *BSRLM*, 24(2), pp69–74.

What the research and classroom experience of the Thinking Together team and teachers involved in its various projects has shown is that the key identifying conditions and features of effective talk are: everyone is encouraged to contribute; everyone listens actively; ideas and opinions are treated with respect; information is shared; challenges are welcomed; reasons are required; contributions build on what has gone before; alternatives are discussed before decisions are taken; the groups work towards agreement before an action is taken; it is possible for participants to change their minds; discussion is understood to be a way of learning.

The students and the computer
A classic feature of classroom talk is the three-part IRF (Initiation, Response, Follow-up) interaction (Sinclair & Coulthard 1975; 1992). In the Thinking Together approach we have developed the notion of IDRF around the computer:

Initiation – by the computer
*D*iscussion – between the students
Response – by the students together
Follow-up – by the computer

Although computers (like teachers) prompt, respond and frame the dialogues with the students, their infinite patience and non-judgmental (inter)face enables this second

---

phase of discussion to become a powerful space in which the students can talk and think their way to a solution of the problem they face. By setting the students to 'play' against the computer, their group work has a clear purpose and reduces the personal tensions within the group itself.

The role of the teacher

Teachers provide a crucial role in modelling appropriate language and behaviour to the students.

Another crucial role for the teacher is that of monitor. Moving around the classroom, the teacher is able to observe points at which an intervention would help, e.g. to check the students' understanding and probe for shifts in thinking.

The teacher here … [can check] … their mathematical strategies and ability to justify their reasoning … Teachers have also found other ways to support the Thinking Together approach by providing students with cue-cards on post-it notes stuck to the computers so that the children can refer to the ground-rules during the lesson.

Analysis

It is clear that in order to ensure purposeful discussion, careful planning must occur. This would suggest that a decision to use ICT has been deliberate, with clear understanding about the learning and conceptual development that the children will engage in while using the ICT.

It also assumes that discussion will not occur in a vacuum, with the teacher's presence needed to facilitate the talk. This will require the teacher to spend part of the mathematics session focusing upon those children using ICT. There is a tendency to assume that the children using ICT will be able to work independently, despite the exhortation of the National Numeracy Strategy (DfEE, 1999, p32) that: *Independent use of computer programmes is usually inappropriate in the daily lesson.*

If this is the case then a change in organisational strategy is required so as to ensure that the planned opportunities are realised. Another element of planning will be the clear identification of the strategies needed to develop the mathematical discussions. This might include identifying key questions or how to model specific processes, along with the recognition of the need for children to be able to practise the collaborative thinking and discussion (Wegerif and Dawes, 2004).

Choosing to use ICT within the mathematics lesson in order to develop these skills provides clear opportunities for the class teacher to develop other thinking skills (McGuinness *et al.*, 2003). These include decision-making, critical thinking, creative thinking, searching for meaning and problem-solving.

If developing children's mathematical communication using ICT as a stimulus and interface is considered valuable, then it is important that the range of software available is analysed along with how it can best be used for the benefit of all the children. The key attributes of a variety of software types are discussed elsewhere (e.g. Poulter and

Basford, 2003; Fox *et al.*, 2000; Sharp *et al.*, 2000; Smith, 1999), but this area requires specific consideration for each class. Other elements related to the use of ICT in this manner also require thought. These include the context in which the learning will take place:

- ICT suite or classroom PC;
- individual, small group, whole class;
- supported or unsupported (is there a role for the teaching assistant?).

Securing engagement

Sharp *et al.* (2000) highlight the attributes of ICT that contribute to teaching and learning. These include interactivity, provisionality, speed and automatic functions along with capacity and range (p4). These elements contribute to the description of ICT as a 'catalyst' (p5) within the learning process. The clear implication is that they help secure engagement of the children in the learning process.

However, a note of caution is expressed, asking whether the software employed within classrooms trivialises learning through the elevation of 'fun'. This concern is extended to make the important point that our pedagogy should not be coerced by the available technology; rather that the technology should be used to enhance the learning opportunities of the children (Fox *et al.*, 2000).

Extract: Passey, D, Rogers, C, Machell, J, and McHugh, G (2004) *The motivational effect of ICT on pupils*. University of Lancaster: DfES.

Motivational impact on learning

The motivational profiles obtained from the quantitative survey demonstrated the existence of a highly positive set of motivational characteristics in the schools in this study. In summary, pupils were characterised, when focusing on working with ICT, by relatively high levels of learning goals and performance approach goals. The analysis of the quantitative data indicated that the forms of motivation arising from ICT use were concerned with learning rather than a mere completion of tasks. Perceptions of learning within classrooms were particularly strong and showed that pupils perceived their classrooms, when using ICT, to be focused very much on the process of learning although many pupils demonstrated anxiety regarding the implications of getting things wrong in front of others, the teacher in particular.

The findings suggested that ICT was helping to draw pupils into more positive modes of motivation. ICT appeared to be offering a means for a range of pupils to envisage success. It enabled pupils to see possible end-points for their work, and to recognise that they could work towards these in order to complete work. However, the use of ICT had to be coupled with learning tasks that were appropriate, and where teaching provided a core of focused pointers (such as where to find appropriate sources, and how to select relevant information).

With a range of ICT equipment, motivational effect did not depend upon motivation related to a single form of ICT. Motivation under these circumstances was often determined by factors concerned with the form of software or learning resource the

---

hardware, and the teaching approach taken. It was reported that, within a positive environment, most pupils enjoyed using ICT (1 out of 200 as exceptions were reported in a number of cases). A concern was that motivation would be short term, associated with 'novelty factors' (interest arising from doing something different or new, with reduced impact after a few weeks). Whilst there were indications of novelty factors being involved in some reported instances, pupils also indicated that their interest was maintained over years of use, both in the cases of software such as writing software and in the presentation offered by interactive whiteboards, for example.

If, as the research suggests the main focus of teacher interest and drive is upon the aspects most commonly reported as leading to positive motivation (engagement, research, writing and editing, and presentation), then internal cognitive aspects of the learning process (aspects such as reasoning, comparing, analysis, evaluating and conceptualising) are being given less attention overall, and may not be supported positively to the same extents currently by ICT. If this pattern applies widely to practice, then it suggests that teachers are driving uses of ICT to support internalisation (the ways in which ideas and knowledge that are presented can be taken into the mind through the senses) and externalisation processes (the ways in which ideas and knowledge in the mind can be related to others through processes such as speaking and writing) more strongly than internal cognitive processes. Motivational impacts and outcomes of learning in terms of attainment therefore, if related, might be expected to manifest themselves in a similar way. If attainment is linked to internal cognition then current practice with ICT will have less impact upon attainment than it does upon other parts of the learning process.

Teaching and learning environments

Where ICT use was focused on both teaching and learning (for example, the use of clusters of equipment to support subject learning and interactive whiteboards to support teaching), the potential for impacts upon motivation appeared to be greater than if there was a single focus upon teaching (for example, in a school where ICT courses were run, without any integration of ICT into other subject learning or teaching). Where used effectively, both teachers and pupils reported that the use of interactive whiteboards was motivating. The features that led to motivational impact were concerned with presentational devices (allowing items to be flashed up, or items to be completed), annotation effects and direct interaction through touch. From a teaching point of view, teachers used these devices to deliver to a whole class, could use the digital content effectively that was available to them, could easily review aspects previously covered, and could increase the pace of lessons to the extent that pupils were aware of this increased pace.

Teachers reported widely that ICT offered them enhanced resources to support learning through teaching. The levels of interaction, the visual quality of resources, the immediacy, the ability to refresh work and to redo it, were all indicated as ways in which ICT could enhance the range of teaching approaches taken. Teachers with interactive whiteboards said that they used features so that pupils could observe, then talk and question to increasing extents. In some schools, teachers indicated that they were expecting more of pupils as a result of ICT being used – whether this was due to a higher pace in lessons, work being done more quickly, aspects of analysis that could be focused upon to greater extents, or work being completed outside school more effectively.

Impact on behaviour

Behaviour in lessons was reported by pupils as being better in most cases when ICT was used, and worse in only a minority of cases. The vast majority of pupils indicated that they enjoyed using ICT in lessons. The only exceptions were cases where ICT was used only in ICT lessons and where access to ICT was felt to be limited. Many teachers reported that ICT was supporting independence of pupil learning.

Impact on specific groups of pupils

Different groups of pupils were found to be gaining in different ways from the use of ICT. ICT used in special schools often enabled communication at a basic and fundamental level. For example, some pupils could not communicate with the external world, either at all, or easily, without the use of ICT-based access devices. The information aspects of ICT were fundamentally important to other groups, such as those who were gifted and talented. The success of those who had worked with pupils at risk was often due to their ability to use communication aspects initially then to move on at appropriate times to information use.

Analysis

The motivational impact of using ICT within the mathematics lesson seems particularly strong. While recognising this, one question that should be considered is the position taken within the extract of the nature of mathematics. Is mathematics portrayed as rather utilitarian in nature, only valuable for its usefulness? Is there not an argument for viewing mathematics as intrinsically interesting (see Chapter 1)?

Papert (1980) asserts that one of the key elements of mathematics is fascination. He argues strongly that mathematics should not be seen as a purely logical process, *a deductive system in which new truths are derived from previously derived truths by means of rigorously reliable rules of inference* (p194). Rather, he highlights the deeply personal nature of mathematics and the involvement of those who study mathematics, which enables the personal responses of fascination when interacting with the subject. In our presentation of mathematical learning to children, are there opportunities to develop a personal response? Is it possible to illustrate creativity or generate fascination about a particular aspect of mathematics?

An example of children developing an intrinsic interest in an aspect of mathematics involves investigating patterns. Picture two able Year 4 children investigating a number sequence and determining the rule to enable accurate calculation of the next number in the sequence. Once they are introduced to the mathematician who discovered the sequence – Fibonnacci – they then spend a great deal of time researching where this special sequence can be observed. This develops into a clear aesthetic mathematical awareness, generating significant pleasure within the children.

Personal response

Having considered the extracts in this chapter, you have a decision to make about whether to use ICT or not.

Consider the following questions in relation to the last time you used ICT within a mathematics lesson.

- How did you last use ICT within a mathematics lesson?
- Why did you use the ICT?
- What was the outcome in terms of:
  - children's learning;
  - your teaching?
- Did you actively consider whether using the ICT would help you to deliver that session more effectively or whether it would enable the children to develop a clearer understanding of the mathematics being taught?

When you are next planning to use ICT in your mathematics session:

- Reflect on how it will impact on your teaching. How will it affect what you do?
- Reflect on how it will affect the children's understanding of the mathematics.
- Then, based on these reflections, make your decision whether to include ICT or not.

Conclusion

Whatever our personal views about ICT are, these are key questions that we need to consider in relation to the teaching and learning of mathematics. As conscious decisions are made about using ICT within teaching mathematics, so:

- what ICT you use in your mathematics teaching will become purposeful;
- why you could use ICT within your mathematics lessons will become evident;
- how ICT can be best used to secure effective teaching and learning will be demonstrated.

The result of making these decisions will have a positive impact on the quality of learning and teaching within primary mathematics.

8 Effective teaching of mathematics

By the end of this chapter you should have:

- reflected on **why** there is a need for a range of different ways of teaching mathematics;
- considered **what** elements are involved in effective mathematics learning;
- identified **how** you might promote children's learning of mathematics in your classroom.

Linking your learning

- DfEE (1999) *The National Numeracy Strategy.* London: DfEE Publications, Introduction.
- Mooney, C, Fletcher, M, Briggs, M and McCullouch, J (2002) *Achieving QTS. Primary mathematics: teaching theory and practice* (2nd edition). Exeter: Learning Matters, Chapters 1, 2 and 3.

Professional Standards for QTS
2.1, 2.4

Introduction

Many elements come together to make an effective lesson but the main criterion for judging a successful lesson is that children's learning has taken place. If you believe that children construct their learning by extending and building on previous learning, then you will probably adopt a constructivist approach. This is dependent on your knowing the prior knowledge of your children so that you can provide the appropriate next step. You cannot assume that all children achieve a good understanding or remember every piece of learning presented to them, so careful monitoring of learning needs to be built into your teaching strategies. Black and Wiliam have extensively researched assessment approaches that enable teachers to increase children's participation in mathematics lessons and thus create situations where data can be observed and collected (Black and Wiliam, 1998; Black *et al.*, 2003). This informs the teacher's decisions about the appropriate work to present to the children in their class. The first extract in this chapter draws on some of Black and Wiliam's work.

Another important aspect of the successful lesson is the style in which it is conducted. The three-part lesson recommended by the National Numeracy Strategy currently predominates in English primary school classrooms. Prior to this many primary schools conducted mathematics lessons by individuals working from textbooks, workcards or worksheets. With the introduction of the Foundation Stage from 3 to 5 years old in England and Wales, Reception classes and Key Stage 1 classes are beginning to draw upon the child-initiated approach which has functioned in many Nursery schools. The second extract by Carol Barnes illustrates the organisation that underpins this approach.

Assessment for learning

This extract is part of a series of published papers centred on research carried out by King's College London with secondary schools in Gravesend. The project has run over a number of years and findings have generated strong evidence for an integrated approach, where formative assessment needs to be inextricably linked to teaching strategies if effective teaching and learning is to take place.

Before you read this extract, read about Black and Wiliam's 10 key principles at **www.qca.org.uk/907.html**.

> **Extract: Black, P and Wiliam, D (2001) 'Inside the black box: Raising standards through classroom assessment'. Available at http://ngfl.northumberland.gov.uk/ keystage3ictstrategy/Assessment/blackbox.pdf**
>
> **The evolution of effective teaching**
> The research studies referred to in the first part of this paper show very clearly that effective programmes of formative assessment involve far more than the addition of a few observations and tests to an existing programme. They require careful scrutiny of all of the main components of a teaching plan. As the argument develops it becomes clear that instruction and formative assessment are indivisible.
>
> To begin at the beginning, the choice of tasks for class and home work is important. Tasks have to be justified in terms of the learning aims that they serve, and they can only work well if opportunities for pupils to communicate their evolving understanding are built into the planning. Discussion, observation of activities, marking of written work, can all be used to provide the opportunities, but it is then important to look at, or listen carefully to, the talk, the writing, the actions through which pupils develop and display the state of their understanding.
>
> - Opportunities for pupils to express their understanding should be designed into any piece of teaching, for this will initiate the interaction whereby formative assessment aids learning.
>
> Discussions, in which pupils are led to talk about their understanding in their own ways, are important aids to improved knowledge and understanding. Dialogue with the teacher provides the opportunity for the teacher to respond to and re-orient the pupil's thinking. However, there are clearly-recorded examples of such discussions where teachers have, quite unconsciously, responded in ways that would inhibit the future learning of a pupil. What the examples have in common is that the teacher is looking for a particular response and lacks the flexibility or the confidence to deal with the unexpected. So the teacher tries to direct the pupil towards giving the expected answer. In manoeuvring the conversation in this way, the teacher seals off any unusual, often thoughtful but unorthodox, attempts by the pupils to work out their own

answers. Over time the pupils get the message – they are not required to think out their own answers. The object of the exercise is to work out, or guess, what answer the teacher expects to see or hear, and then express it so that the teaching can proceed.

A particular feature of the talk between teacher and pupils is the asking of questions by the teacher. This natural and direct way of checking on learning is often unproductive. One common problem is that teachers do not allow enough quiet time so that pupils can think out and offer an answer. Where, as often happens, a teacher answers her or his own question after only two or three seconds, and where a minute (say) of silent thought is not tolerable, there is no possibility that a pupil can think out what to say. There are then two consequences. One is that, because the only questions that can produce answers in such a short time are questions of fact, these predominate. The other is that pupils don't even try to think out a response – if you know that the answer, or another question, will come along in a few seconds, there is no point in trying. It is also common that only a few pupils in a class answer teachers' questions. The rest then leave it to these few, knowing that they cannot respond as quickly and being unwilling to risk making mistakes in public. So the teacher, by lowering the level of questions and by accepting answers from a few, can keep the lesson going but is actually out of touch with the understanding of most of the class – the question-answer dialogue becomes a ritual, one in which all connive and thoughtful involvement suffers.

There are several ways to break this particular cycle. They involve giving pupils time to respond, asking them to discuss their thinking in pairs or in small groups so that a respondent is speaking on behalf of others, giving pupils a choice between different possible answers and asking them to vote on the options, asking all to write down an answer and then reading out a selected few, and so on. What is essential is that any dialogue should evoke thoughtful reflection in which all pupils can be encouraged to take part, for only then can the formative process start to work.

- The dialogue between pupils and a teacher should be thoughtful, reflective, focused to evoke and explore understanding, and conducted so that all pupils have an opportunity to think and to express their ideas.

Class tests, and tests or other exercises set for homework, are also important means to promote feedback. A good test can be a learning as well as a testing occasion. It is better to have frequent short tests than infrequent and longer ones. Any new learning should first be tested within about a week of first encounter, but tests more frequent than this are counter-productive. The quality of the test items, i.e. their relevance to the main learning aims and their clear communication to the pupil, needs scrutiny. Good questions are hard to generate and teachers should collaborate, and draw – critically – on outside sources, to collect such questions.

Given questions of good quality, it is then essential to ensure the quality of the feedback. Research studies have shown that if pupils are given only marks or grades, they do not benefit from the feedback on their work. The worst scenario is one in which some pupils get low marks this time, they got low marks last time, they expect to get low marks next time, and this is accepted as part of a shared belief between them and their teacher that they are just not clever enough. Feedback has been shown to improve learning where it gives each pupil specific guidance on strengths and weaknesses, preferably without any overall marks. Thus, the way in which test results are reported back to pupils so that they can identify their own strengths and weaknesses is a critical feature. Pupils must be given the means and opportunities to work with evidence of their difficulties. Thus, for formative purposes a test at the end of a block or module of teaching is pointless in that it is too late to work with the results.

- Tests and homework exercises can be an invaluable guide to learning, but the exercises must be clear and relevant to learning aims. The feedback on them should give each pupil guidance on how to improve, and each must be given opportunity and help to work at the improvement.

All these points make clear that there is no one simple way to improve formative assessment. What is common to them is that a teacher's approach should start by being realistic-confronting the question 'Do I really know enough about the understanding of my pupils to be able to help each of them?'

Analysis

Black and Wiliam advocate the altering of practice to accommodate greater pupil participation. This allows children to demonstrate their understanding through the use of their knowledge. It also gives the teacher an opportunity to observe and discuss with children the mathematics they are engaged in. In this way the teacher can collect data to inform his or her planning. What strategies could you use to get children to discuss their mathematics in class? Consider how you would include these in your lesson plans.

Questioning is a significant teacher strategy. Black and Wiliam identify a weak pattern of questioning where the teacher almost expects the children to guess what he or she is thinking. What effect does this have on the children? They also refer to allowing 'quiet time' or developing greater 'response time' (Rowe, 1974). Jeffcoat et al. (2004) identify a range of question types including those that require children to remember pieces of information, those that require explanation and those that draw upon knowledge to construct new thinking. Consider what type of response you would get from using questions which contain the following interrogative commands: choose, why, what would happen if, justify, apply, who, where, compare.

Dweck (1989) found in her research that if grades and written comments are given, children tend to pay attention only to the grades and ignore the comments. She also contends that grades promote externally motivated children who are less likely to develop as independent learners. These she links to children who develop performance-related goals and those who develop learning goals. What suggestions do Black and Wiliam make to ensure that children do utilise the written feedback, and how could you accommodate their findings in your own lessons?

An effective pedagogy for teaching mathematics in the Early Years

Before reading this extract, you may wish to read some of the Effective Provision of Pre-school Education (EPPE) research at **www.ioe.ac.uk/cdl/eppe/pdfs/eppe.brief2503.pdf**

Extract: Barnes, C (2005) 'Too much teaching'. *Mathematics Teaching,* **190: 23–5.**
Copyright © Christine Barnes, Association of Teachers of Mathematics.

Do we spend too much time teaching our children and not enough time watching them learn? At a recent conference in Cornwall many teachers and other professionals listened to Iram Siraj-Blatchford talking about her large-scale research project, *Researching effective pedagogy in the early years* (EPPE) research) [DfES, 2002]. She spoke particularly about the balance between adult-directed and child-initiated play in the foundation stage. For many teachers this is a particularly difficult problem, especially in mathematics, as they feel that they need to follow the basic structure of the daily mathematics lesson as used in Key Stages 1 and 2. Even when they do find time for children to initiate activities for themselves, they are not sure what children are learning as they rarely have time to listen to and talk with children as they play. But as Siraj-Blatchford notes from her research, it is only when adults become involved with children's play in a planned and focused way, encouraging shared thinking, that children's learning really moves forward [DfES, 2003].

Last year I observed a student working with a group of my reception class children. In a tightly structured activity, the children were throwing dice and finding which Cuisenaire (Colour Factor) rods corresponded to the numbers shown on their dice. The student became frustrated, and remarked that many children 'co-operated' for a short time but then wanted to go, or played with the rods in their own way. With his inexperience, what he failed to notice was that when the children were not 'on task' but playing more freely, they were finding out for themselves exactly the kinds of things he wanted them to learn. As we discussed afterwards, had the children been allowed to play, with skilled questioning to direct and focus their thinking, the learning may have been better, and certainly the children would have shown more interest and deeper concentration on the activity.

In fact, I have become increasingly committed to spending time observing and becoming involved in children's play, especially in mathematics. In the Foundation Stage so much of what children need to learn is expressed in terms of 'talking about' aspects of mathematics or using appropriate vocabulary. These skills can be very well developed through playing with children, rather than through structured activities. The more time I take to play with children, the more I find they have already grasped many of the concepts and mathematical words I was planning to teach them. Moreover, it is through play that children's misconceptions (for instance that bigger things are always heavier) can be identified and addressed in ways that are meaningful to the children. Observing children as they play often suggests structured as well as play activities that would be a beneficial way of introducing new concepts or practising developing skills. Such observations can form the basis of a useful plenary session or a whole class introductory session the next day.

There were several occasions when this approach was helpful as we observed the children playing in our 'fruit and vegetable shop' earlier this year. We quickly noticed that when asked for seven potatoes, a few children carefully counted out the required number. At this stage in the year, however, most children would count out all of the potatoes in the basket, and then become confused as there were more than seven! This formed the basis of some structured counting sessions, working with small numbers of fruit and vegetables. Some children learned how to count more accurately, using a range of simple strategies, while others learned how to make adjustments, for instance putting one potato back if eight had been accidentally picked out. We noticed the same thing when children were counting out money to pay for their goods. In our structured sessions, we responded to this problem by pricing all of the items very cheaply (1p to 5p) and giving the children only five pennies to spend. We asked them each to choose and buy one item, picking out the correct number of pennies from their purses. In this situation several more of the children began to count more accurately. They were particularly pleased to find that after spending 3p, they still had 2p left to buy something else, so careful counting had really paid off! Moreover, as other adults in the class joined in the children's free play in the shop over the next days and weeks, they were more aware of the children's skills and encouraged them to put them into practice in this 'real' situation.

So what might be an effective way of teaching young children mathematics? In QCA's *Curriculum guidance for the foundation stage* [QCA/DfEE, 2000], the term 'teaching' is deemed to include all aspects of a teacher's role, including planning the learning environment and supporting and extending children's play, learning and development. The EPPE research shows that children learn best individually and in small groups, rather than in whole class situations. This could be because in the Foundation Stage whole class teaching is not targeted sufficiently towards individual children's needs: we are teaching some children things they already know, whilst others are not ready for this information, and yet others do not have the personal, social and emotional skills to sit still and listen in a large group when they are only four years old. Perhaps, then, we need to keep our whole group sessions at the beginning and end of the sessions short, the main aim to being to draw together some of the children's play experiences, unpicking the mathematical learning a little, and introducing appropriate new vocabulary. This will give the children (and adults) more time for both adult-initiated and particularly child-initiated play.

It's important too, that these periods of self-initiated play are not too fragmented. Teachers often complain they have so much to get through each day that the children don't have extended and uninterrupted time for high quality play to develop. One teacher recently remarked:

> It just starts to get interesting then it's 'tidy up time' – time to come and do some maths all together on the carpet, when actually they were already doing mathematics in their play.

Children need time to become deeply involved in their play, and this is something that really strikes everyone who visits the Reggio Emilia pre-schools in Italy [Abbott and Nutbrown, 2001] where children may spend days building an elaborate structure with blocks, supported by adult intervention from time to time but otherwise uninterrupted. Play is not something to be fitted in when the 'work' is done. For young children, play is their work and this is how things should be.

Thankfully the now statutory Foundation Stage gives teachers the freedom to reorganise our time so that children and adults call play together.

Analysis

Throughout this extract there is the recognition that there is a tension between more formal ways of delivering the curriculum as currently promoted by the National Numeracy Strategy (1999) and the way young children learn. How does Barnes justify that learning is taking place when children appear to be 'off-task' in a more formal group learning situation?

What key factors move children's learning forward within play situations? Barnes refers to 'child-initiated play' and 'adult-initiated play'. What elements does each of these have and what differences are there in learning opportunities? Also consider the difference between free play and children playing in a structured environment.

Analyse the illustration of the shopping experience to show how planning could facilitate learning about money over a short period of time. This will illustrate how Barnes and her team respond to the children's needs. This sequence of planning and teaching is a good illustration of the assessment for learning being promoted by Black and Wiliam in the previous extract.

A key need, according to Barnes, is the development of vocabulary in early mathematics. It is normal for adults to use vocabulary that children understand but do not use themselves. How can adults help children to assimilate this new vocabulary? Wood (1987) refers to 'scaffolding learning'. Indicate what situations you could plan into an Early Years' mathematics curriculum to enable adults to use this approach.

Why does Barnes consider whole-class teaching a less suitable learning environment for Foundation Stage children than small group or individual work? Is there a role for whole-class teaching in the Foundation Stage and, if so, when would you use it? Justify your answer.

Personal response

In your experience as a learner and as a teacher, consider your most memorable mathematics lessons. Are these positive or negative feelings? For many people there is a sense of failure linked to learning mathematics. This could be because people continue to do more and more mathematics until the point where it becomes too difficult to understand and they are forced into a strategy of learning formulae by heart in the hope they will be able to apply them. As the subject develops, it is dependent on symbols and abstract ideas which express numerical and spatial relationships. Consider the elements of successful past experiences both as a teacher and as a student. Was the mathematics understood? Was the context interesting? Did the teacher explain the mathematics well? Was the teacher sympathetic to the students' difficulties? Was there a sense of progress?

Conclusion

Both the extracts in this chapter consider the effectiveness of children's learning through the actions of the teacher. If a teacher is to provide an effective learning environment, the first question they must ask themselves is, 'Is learning taking place?'

If the answer is yes, then the next question to ask is, 'Can I create a more effective learning environment?'

This can only happen if the teacher is prepared to reflect on their own practice. In this chapter the focus has been on only two aspects of teaching: formative assessment and a style of teaching for the Early Years. There are many aspects of teaching and children's learning that can be evaluated and many strategies employed to give children a better and more successful learning experience.

9 Catering for a range of mathematical abilities

By the end of this chapter you should have:

- reflected on **why** children are sometimes excluded from the mathematics curriculum;
- considered **what** your own perceptions are in relation to the issues of inclusion in mathematics;
- identified **how** all children might be included in mathematics learning.

Linking your learning

- DfEE (1999) *The National Numeracy Strategy*. London: DfEE Publications.
- Mooney, C, Fletcher, M, Briggs, M and McCullouch, J (2002) *Achieving QTS. Primary mathematics: teaching theory and practice* (2nd edition). Exeter: Learning Matters, Chapters 10 and 11.

Professional Standards for QTS
1.1, 3.1.1, 3.1.2, 3.1.3, 3.3.1

Introduction

This chapter considers how all children of whatever ability can be included in mathematics lessons. When considering inclusion within mathematics, you should remember that many children may feel excluded from mathematics at one time or another in their school career. Children can be excluded, not necessarily because they have particular special educational needs, but because they do not always find mathematics in school accessible.

Children (and adults) think about mathematical problems and processes in a myriad of different ways, and this can make mathematics difficult for teachers to teach and for children to learn. These difficulties may mean that at times a number of children are excluded from lessons because they are unable to develop their understanding of the concepts being taught. There are a variety of reasons for the difficulties that arise within mathematical learning. One reason that children experience exclusion can be that the teacher's level of mathematical subject knowledge is insufficient. If a teacher's understanding of a mathematical concept is unclear, he or she may be unable to follow a child's thought processes, which will hinder the teacher's efforts to help the child to a satisfactory understanding.

Furthermore, a teacher's lack of confidence in mathematics can lead him or her to depend on scripted input, to discourage discussion and to rely on children's worksheets for practice. Mathematics taught in this way tends to stress standardised procedures at the expense of the children's own thinking, understanding and independence. This in turn discourages children from making their own decisions about the way in which they might tackle and record a particular problem and prevents them from developing, expressing and exchanging their own ideas. Thus a child who does not understand and/or cannot remember the taught processes or algorithms can be excluded. A less formal approach, on the other hand, not only allows children to question and express ideas in their own way, but their *errors and misconceptions may be identified more readily through informal and idiosyncratic working* (Anghileri, 2001, p18). Opportunities for the inclusion of all children are more likely to occur when the teacher has been able to identify the children's understanding.

Another reason for the exclusion of some children from mathematics lessons is that their mathematics experiences outside school can be very different from the expectations of mathematics within school. It is not always easy for children to use their informal knowledge, such as scoring in games, filling containers or shopping, as a foundation for their school mathematics and they may not see the connections between the home and school situations. Outside-school mathematical knowledge can be underestimated or go unrecognised by the teacher (Aubrey, 1994, 1997) and she or he may not make the connections between informal and formal knowledge. This may lead to children who otherwise have a secure informal understanding of mathematical concepts, being unable to access the formal school mathematics curriculum. Planning is the key to ensuring the quality of access for all children, and all will progress better if the teacher is able to stress the links between what they already know and what they are to learn rather than emphasising what they do not understand.

On top of the general considerations outlined above, there are a number of more specific, identifiable reasons why children might be excluded from mathematics. All schools will have their own particular difficulties and challenges and most classes of children will be mixed in terms of social and cultural backgrounds. Many classrooms will include children with special educational needs, children with physical disabilities or medical problems, children of ethnic minority groups including travellers, refugees and asylum seekers, and/or children with a variety of first languages other than English. There will also be children whose mathematical understanding is above average and for whom the curriculum can be undemanding. The challenge for teachers is to include all the children in their class in the mathematical learning that takes place there.

This chapter on inclusion will allow you to examine some of the literature concerning two of the groups of children for whom special provision may need to be made. These two groups comprise those who find mathematics particularly demanding or even inaccessible and those who find the mathematics curriculum undemanding and unchallenging. It will allow you to examine particularly some of the problems of access to the mathematics curriculum encountered by children with special educational needs and by the mathematically gifted and able.

Before you read the following extracts, you should refer to DfES (2001) *Guidance to support pupils with dyslexia and dyscalculia, Guidance to support pupils with hearing impairment, Guidance to support pupils with speech and language difficulties, Guidance to support pupils with visual impairment*. Available at **www.standards.dfes. gov.co.uk/numeracy/communities/inclusion**

Mathematics and special educational needs

This extract is part of a lecture given at the Association of Teachers of Mathematics (ATM) 2002 Easter conference entitled 'Mathematics is special'. The author of this paper sets out to explore the possibility that mathematics teachers and special educators have much in common and that the perception of people outside education is that both disciplines involve unrecognised difficulties and ultimate failure.

Before you read this extract, read Bottle, G and the Primary Mathematics Team at Canterbury Christ Church University (2005) 'Equal opportunities and special educational needs in mathematics', in *Teaching mathematics in the primary school*. London: Continuum.

Extract: Visser, J (2002) 'Mathematics, inclusion and pupils'. *Mathematics Teaching 179, Easter Conference Supplement,* **June, pp110–12.**

Mathematicians

Owning up in a social setting to being a teacher of mathematics can be greeted either by stunned silence, by a cathartic outpouring or by an admission that the questioner has mathophobia. Teachers of children with SEN have similar reactions: stunned silence not because the questioner believes themselves to be faced by a superior being but embarrassment because he or she has no point of reference to engage further or a cathartic outpouring because they, or a near relative, have a special educational need that was not recognised or dealt with entirely appropriately.

Special educators and mathematicians are also often on the margins of education. As Gates (2001) explains:

> too many children's experience of mathematics is a daily experience of continued failure and irrelevance.

Mathematics is seen too often as a tool to other aspirations rather than an aspiration in itself. Few pupils see themselves as mathematicians and fewer still aspire to be a mathematician. In a society where aspirational goals for many pupils lie within the arts, sport, service industries, being a mathematician is not a sexy career to pursue! Like teachers of mathematics, teachers of pupils with SEN are often viewed as a breed apart from other colleagues with their own 'special magic dust' to be directed at a group of pupils whose diversity has set them apart. Mathematicians are largely required by other subject colleagues to ensure that pupils can use mathematics within their subjects. Likewise, special educators are required to ensure that pupils with SEN can engage in the learning process of a broad and balanced curriculum.

The recently revised code of practice for SEN has pointed to the fallacies in the above perceptions by emphasising that all teachers are teachers of pupils with special educational needs. It was the Cockcroft Report which stated the need for all teachers to be aware of the mathematics in their subject areas and, therefore, that all were teachers of mathematics. Within the fields of mathematics and special education there is still some way to go to ensure that teachers focus on teaching and learning strategies (the 'of' teaching), and have the subject knowledge to support this effectively (the 'what' of teaching). The emphasis remains upon being a 'mathematics' or 'special educational' teacher rather than a teacher of mathematics or for pupils with SEN.

Mathematics is often perceived as a rigidly hierarchical subject where one concept must be understood before another can be taught. It is also seen as a subject where ability grouping is important if high standards are to be achieved and the most able are to achieve their potential. The net result of this approach is the feeling of exclusion which many pupils experience in mathematics. They may be placed in a mainstream school, but are they included?

The issue of inclusion is not just a policy imposed on education because of national and international treaties and legislation, nor is it the acceptance of pupils with disabilities into our schools and classes. It is how each teacher works with the pupils in his or her class in such a manner that each individual feels included. To achieve this requires the reflective practitioner asking questions about pupils' learning and using the answers to inform their teaching. It is about:

- pace
- relevance
- strategies and
- use of resources.

It requires a shift in teachers' attitudes towards special educational needs. From perceiving SEN as defined within a child's 'condition', where the child's potential is at best slow progress along a linear hierarchical body of knowledge and the child's achievement is limited by the teacher's perceptional concentration upon the disability; to one where teachers embrace the diverse needs of individuals within their class, looking to build upon their strengths in learning.

Such teachers do exist and no doubt readers of this article count themselves among them. The teaching of mathematics has undergone radical changes as witnessed by authors such as Leonie and Ward. Yet it appears the challenges I outline above are echoed in the authors who have contributed to Gates (2001) and others such as Watson. If we want an inclusive society then one of its roots will lie in the way teachers engender the inclusion of pupils in their schools. The teacher of mathematics can contribute to that inclusive society.

Analysis

In the first part of this paper Visser includes a quote attributed to Gates (2001), which explains that *too many children's experience of mathematics is a daily experience of continued failure and irrelevance.* Consider this view. Does it sum up, or differ from, your own experiences of mathematics?

Visser's aim within this paper is to highlight the commonalities between a child learning mathematics and a child who has special educational needs. He believes that mathematics is generally understood as a rigidly hierarchical subject. Is this the view that you have of mathematics? Why does Visser criticise this view? Visser also asserts that the way in which many people perceive the potential of children with special educational needs is a slow progression along a linear hierarchical body of knowledge. He postulates that this is not a helpful way of defining children's mathematical learning or the learning of children with special educational needs and believes that, common to both mathematics and special educational needs, it is the responsibility of teachers not just to take children through a hierarchy of knowledge but to *embrace the diverse needs of individuals within their class* (Visser, 2002, p3).

Personal response

Any child may, at times, feel excluded from the mathematics being taught and the need to provide support for diverse needs is true of any mathematics lesson with any group of children. Examine your own mathematical experiences. Have you ever felt excluded from a mathematics lesson? What may have been the reason for this? Draw on your reading from other chapters in this book to identify how you might help all children to be included in mathematics lessons.

Visser (2002) believes that mathematics is a difficult subject in its own right, but if a child has special educational needs this makes it doubly difficult for them to participate. Visser goes on to argue that unless the general perceptions surrounding mathematics and special educational needs can be changed then there is little hope of inclusion becoming a reality in the classroom. Think about a child you know who has special educational needs or has experienced difficulties with mathematics. How might the problems of that child be minimised within mathematics lessons so that he or she is able to participate fully?

Inclusion and mathematics

This extract is from an article in which the author reflects on her reading and experience to explore the school culture, school policy and school practice of one school in order to consider factors that can help to support inclusive learning.

Before reading this extract, you may wish to access the DfES Standards website at **www.standards.dfes.gov.co.uk/numeracy/communities/inclusion** and reading the *Guidance to support pupils with visual impairment*.

Extract: Corbett, J (2001) 'Teaching approaches which support inclusive education: A connective pedagogy'. *British Journal of Special Educational Needs*, **28**, June: 55–9.

School practice
One of the things I learnt in this project was that differentiation means using many teaching styles and sharing specialist skills. There is a real commitment to including all learners which involves using diverse strategies and working at many different levels on whole-class tasks. Staff recognise that children learn in many different ways and that

some prefer visual rather than oral stimulus. Individual achievement is the goal. As the SENCO says:

> This means ensuring that children are all working on something at which they can gain success and move forward at their own level so that they can take the next step.

This can apply to a specific child with an evident disability, for example:

> A four year-old blind boy, with his LSA, is participating in the numeracy hour. The teacher is working with six children on the carpet to do a session on 'Recognising Shapes'. She holds up a picture which has raised spongy shapes of triangles, squares and circles which the boy can feel. It is a feely-shape, large book (an inclusive source). The teacher gets the other children to interact with him (e.g. passing around a penny when they are exploring round shapes). The group were helped to see the shape by the teacher drawing it on his hand. (field-notes)

Through considering ways in which resources and teaching approaches can include learners with disabilities, all the group can benefit, as what works well for this child may also be very helpful to others who find the interactive learning is reinforcing.

One of the aspects of teaching and learning which really impressed me was that teachers are sufficiently confident to share their experiments in adopting new strategies with the students, as in this example:

> Numeracy hour with 10 and 11 year olds: all the class have been given a set of number cards, from I to 10, tied together with a string. They are used as a visual aid. When the teacher says '3 × 12', they have to select from their number cards and hold up 3 and 6 in front of them, not shout it out. This is the first time the teacher has tried this approach. She is very open with her pupils about the methods, saying 'This is supposed to be a good idea. I'm not convinced of it.' Her reflections were because the children focused on the cards rather than on the thinking process. Some children liked them as they gave visual clues and their style was more visual. (field-notes)

The open attitude to sharing the learning experience means that the students participate as active learners, illustrating how they learn best and what they find most helpful. Teachers listen and learn. When a boy, on stage 3 of the *Code of Practice* because of his challenging behaviour, asked to go into the adjoining empty room to work on his own with the specialist teacher, this request was complied with. His choice was respected. At other times, the class meet together in Circle Time to decide how they will respond as a group to specific behaviours from an individual who is creating difficulty for them. They are constantly made aware that they are active participants in the school community and that their views are taken seriously.

I saw much teaching that I would regard as exceptionally skilled in any circumstances. There is a real effort made to involve the learners, to create situations in which they can meet with success and to build on their existing level of knowledge. LSAs are well briefed by teachers and work co-operatively to ensure that there are no individuals who are isolated from the group and not participating in any meaningful way. So many skilful strategies have been learnt and adapted by the teaching team that it is hard to say where mainstream teaching ends and specialist teaching begins. I felt that they had skilled themselves up to be able to accommodate the needs of children with Asperger's syndrome, autism, Down's syndrome, William's syndrome and Attention Deficit Hyperactivity Disorder, who were included within their school population. There is a will to learn and a capacity to be highly flexible.

Analysis

This extract was written as a discussion of the findings of a small-scale research project, looking at how inclusion could really work in a school. The author identifies the importance of the common vision within the school that describes what they believe inclusive education to be. As the piece develops, the author tries to tease out what it is about the school culture, policy and practice that helps to create an inclusive community. The extract looks particularly at the school's practice that ensures inclusion in mathematics lessons. In the extract there is an observation of a mathematics lesson in a Reception class at the school. Read the extract carefully and consider what it was about the session with the four-year-old blind boy that made it so successful. Was it the provision of suitable resources or was it more than this?

Personal response

In the article from which this extract is drawn, the author describes the school chosen for focus of her study as working successfully as an inclusive school, and later in the extract she describes the teachers as exceptionally skilled. What do you consider were the main reasons for their success? Write down a list of words and phrases that exemplify the attitude of the school; for example, 'respect'. How might consideration of this article affect the ways in which you plan for mathematics lessons in the future?

Inclusion and the able child

Have you ever considered that the mathematically able child might feel excluded from mathematics lessons? They may find mathematics undemanding and unchallenging, which may lead them to be unwilling to join in mathematics lessons.

Before you read this extract, you may wish to read the National Numeracy Strategy section on mathematically gifted and able children.

Extract, from Eyre, D and McClure, L (2002) *Curriculum provision for gifted and talented in the primary school, English, mathematics and ICT.* **London: NACE/Fulton, pp64–89.**

What do we mean when we describe a child as being able in mathematics?
How might a child be defined as able in maths? Trafton (1981) suggests that there are three groups of pupils who can be described as 'mathematically able'; those who:

- learn content well and perform accurately but find difficulty when taught at a faster pace or at a deeper conceptual level;

- learn more content at deeper level, reason well, are capable of solving more complex problems that the average student;
- are highly talented or precocious because they work at the level of a student several years older and seem to need little or no formal instruction. They learn at a faster rate and deal well with sophisticated content and problems.

These three types could conveniently be called more able, most able and exceptionably able, although these are not discrete categories. Indeed, most writers (e.g. Kennard 1996, Kruteski 1976) prefer to consider mathematical ability as a selection of particular characteristics drawn from a wide menu. The particular recipe of characteristics differs from individual to individual. Another model others have used is a continuum ranging from able to exceptional. Throughout the chapter are the case studies of primary aged pupils working in maths. You may wish to consider where you would place them along the continuum (see Figure 1).

| All students | Able students | Highly able and specialised talents | Outstanding talents | Most exceptional talents |

Figure 1 Continuum of ability

Ability changes over time

One of the things we know about primary children is that their abilities change and are expressed differently over time. Identifying able mathematicians at 5 is different from identifying them at say 11, partly because they have fewer skills to exhibit their abilities and partly because their abilities may change. The child who is extremely good at oral number work at 5 may perhaps be benefiting from much parental involvement. The difference between him and his peers may not be sustained when his peers have had a chance to catch up with him.

However, Bloom's three phases of giftedness ... can be recognised in children of mathematical ability. A broad framework into which researchers have attempted to insert more detail is provided by the three phases of early years' fascination with order and pattern which develops into mastery and subsequently into creative activity.

Able Pupils and the National Numeracy Strategy

In an analysis of able pupils working within the daily mathematics session, the Excellence in Cities national training programme (DFEE 2000) adds that able mathematicians frequently:

- Are enthusiastic about and enjoy discussing mathematics, both abstract and concrete;
- Show an ability to estimate and predict accurately;
- Show persistence and flexibility in their search for solutions;

- Apply the same useful approaches to problem solving across a range of contexts;
- Perceive the practical and everyday applications of mathematics;
- Are able to describe, explain and justify the methods they use;
- May have strengths in different areas of maths;
- Are 'holistic' in their approaches to problems, e.g. not necessarily showing exceptional ability with calculations but having an awareness of problems as a whole, or the importance of their choice of processes.

The last characteristic is one upon which several other writers have commented (Koshy 2001). The numeracy strategy emphasises fluency and accuracy in mental and written calculation. Some very able pupils may be unexceptional in this area, preferring to work on the 'bigger picture'. Assessment procedures such as SATs contribute to the identification of competent mathematicians who may be content when addressing computational activities but become unsettled by anything which requires thinking about mathematics in a different way. On the other hand, children may not be identified as anything other that very competent unless they are provided with additional opportunities to work at mathematics at a deeper and more complex level. It is unlikely that pupils will exhibit talent in, for example, describing, explaining and justifying their choice of method if they are not given the opportunity to do so. Similarly, small children who are told how to sort their toys may not exhibit the exceptional ability they would have shown had they been allowed to choose their own criteria for sorting. Teachers also need to be aware that high mathematical ability may be masked by a lack of ability in presentation skills, in verbalising or in working cooperatively.

Analysis

This extract examines the ways in which the able mathematician may be recognised in the classroom and how the needs of children so identified might be met. The author identifies three broad categories that might describe able children but goes on to explain that these categories are not discrete but rather exist as a continuum of ability as shown in Figure 1 of the extract. Can you identify a child that you know who might be described as an able mathematician? Where might that child fit along the continuum of ability? How would you ensure that a child who is identified as mathematically able is not excluded from mathematics lessons?

The extract also includes a summary of the characteristics of the able mathematician as identified from the analysis carried out by the Excellence in Cities National Training Programme (DfEE, 2000). Apply these characteristics to a child that you know. How do these criteria fit the child?

The extract explains that some children with high ability may be unable or unwilling to show workings within their mathematics recording. What constraints might such a child find? In what ways might a child's ability to 'know' the answer restrict their participation in mathematics lessons? How might you overcome these problems?

Personal response

Consider observations that you may have carried out of children learning mathematics in school. Which children do you consider might have been excluded in mathematics lessons?

Children within any class will demonstrate a range of needs within their mathematics learning. In a class that you know, think about the range of the children's needs. How do children's needs affect their mathematical learning and/or ability to respond to the curriculum? Consider how these needs are supported and whether special measures are taken to ensure that all children have the opportunity to contribute to mathematics lessons. Are all children given autonomy and the right to be independent and in control of their own mathematical learning?

Many class teachers group their children broadly into three groups so that they can differentiate the mathematics to suit their needs. For a class with which you are familiar, consider how the grouping was decided. Are the children grouped because of their mathematical ability, for example, or are there some other criteria by which children are assigned?

Conclusion

All three extracts in this chapter have considered the issues surrounding the inclusion of all children in mathematics lessons and activity and highlight that it is the teacher's responsibility to overcome any barriers that there might be to the children's learning. If a teacher is to include all children in mathematics learning, then it is important that he or she is aware of the possible reasons for exclusion and is proactive in making sure that all children have the opportunity to engage in mathematics that is accessible to them. Full inclusion can be achieved by providing the environment and/or the special tools that children may require and to match the mathematics curriculum to their individual needs.

References

Abbott, L and Nutbrown, C (2001) *Experiencing Reggio Emilia*. Buckingham: Open University Press.

Anghileri, J (1997) 'Uses of counting in multiplication and division', in Thompson, I (ed) *Teaching and learning early number*. Buckingham: Open University Press, pp41-51.

Anghileri, J (1999) 'Issues in teaching multiplication and division', in Thompson, I (ed) *Issues in teaching numeracy in primary schools*. Buckingham: Open University Press, pp184-94.

Anghileri, J (2000) *Teaching number sense*. London: Continuum.

Anghileri, J (2001) 'Development of division strategies for Year 5 pupils in ten English schools', *British Educational Research Journal* vol. 27 no. 1.

Anghileri, J (2001) 'A study of progression in written calculation strategies for division'. *Support for Learning*, 16(1):17-22.

Askew, M (1993) 'Bug detectives'. *Junior Education*, May.

Askew, M (1997) 'It ain't (just) what you do: Effective teachers of numeracy', in Thomson, I (ed) *Issues in teaching numeracy in primary schools*. Buckingham: Open University Press, pp91-102.

Askew, M (2003) 'Word problems: Cinderellas or wicked witches?', in Thompson, I (ed) *Enhancing primary mathematics teaching*. Maidenhead: Open University Press.

Askew, M and Wiliam, D (1995) Recent research in mathematics education. London: HMSO.

Askew, M, Brown, M, Johnson, D, Rhodes, V and Wiliam, D (1997) *Effective teachers of numeracy: Report of a study carried out for the Teacher Training Agency*. London: King's College, University of London.

Atkinson, S (1992) *Mathematics with reason*. Oxford: Hodder and Stoughton.

Aubrey, C (1994) *The role of subject knowledge in the early years of schooling*. London: Falmer Press.

Aubrey, C (1997) *Mathematics teaching in the early years: An investigation of teachers' subject knowledge*. London: Falmer Press.

Aubrey, C (1999) *Developmental Approach to Early Numeracy*. Birmingham: Questions.

Barnes, C (2005) 'Too much reading', *Mathematics Teaching* no. 190, Association of Teachers of Mathematics.

Bills, C, Bills, E, Mason, J and Watson, A (2004) *Thinkers: a collection of activities to provoke mathematical thinking*. Derby: ATM.

Black, P and Wiliam, D (1998) *Inside the black box: Raising standards through classroom assessment*. London: School of Education, King's College.

Black, P, Harrison, C, Lee, C, Marshall, B and Wiliam, D (2003) *Assessment for learning: Putting it into practice*. Buckingham: Open University Press.

Blinko, J (2004) 'Mathematics in context'. *Mathematics Teaching*, 188:3-9.

Boaler, J (2000) *Experiencing school mathematics*. Buckingham: Open University Press.

Bottle, G and the Primary Mathematics Team at Canterbury Christ Church University (2005) 'Equal opportunities and special educational needs in mathematics', in *Teaching mathematics in the primary school*. London: Continuum.

Brissenden, T (1998) *Talking about mathematics*. Oxford: Blackwell.

Clarke, S (2001) Unlocking formative assessment. London: Hodder and Stoughton.

Clarke, S (2003) Enriching feedback in the primary classroom. London: Hodder and Stoughton.

Cockcroft, W (1982) Mathematics counts. London: HMSO.

Cooper, B (1998) 'Assessing National Curriculum mathematics in England: Exploring children's interpretation of Key Stage 2 tests in clinical interviews'. Educational Studies in Mathematics, 35:19-49.

Cooper, B and Dunne, M (2000) Assessing children's mathematical knowledge. Buckingham: Open University Press.

Cooper, B and Harries, T (2002) 'Children's responses to contrasting 'realistic' mathematics: Just how realistic are children ready to be?', Educational Studies in Mathematics, 49:1-23.

Corbett, J (2001) 'School practice', British Journal of Special Education, vol. 28 no. 2.

Cox, M (1997) 'Identification of the changes in attitude and pedagogical practices needed to enable teachers to use information technology in the school curriculum', in Passey, D and Samways, B (eds) Information technology: Supporting change through teacher education. London: Chapman and Hall.

De Corte, E and Verschaffel, L (1987) 'The effect of semantic structure on first graders' solution strategies of elementary addition and subtraction word problems'. Journal for Research in Mathematics Education, 18:363-81.

De Feu, C (2001) 'Naming and shaming'. Mathematics in School, May: 2-8.

DES and Welsh Office (1988) Task Group on Assessment and Testing (TEGAT). London: DES (the original recommendations for the assessment of the National Curriculum).

DfEE (1999) The National Numeracy Strategy. London: DfEE Publications.

DfES (2001) Guidance to support pupils with dyslexia and dyscalculia, Guidance to support pupils with hearing impairment, Guidance to support pupils with speech and language difficulties, Guidance to support pupils with visual impairment. Available at www.standards.dfes.gov.uk/numeracy/communities/inclusion

DfES (2001) Special Educational Needs Code of Practice. Nottinghamshire: DfES Publications.

Dweck, C S (1989) 'Motivation', in Lesgold, A and Glaser, R (eds) Foundation for psychology of education. Hillsdale, NJ: Laurence Erlbaum.

Edwards, D and Mercer, N (1987) Common knowledge: The development of understanding in the classroom. London: Methuen.

Eyre, D and McClure, L (2001) Curriculum provision for the gifted and talented in the primary school: English, mathematics, Science and ICT. London: David Fulton.

Floyd, A (1981) Developing mathematical thinking. Addison Wesley/Open University Press.

Fox, B, Montague-Smith, A and Wilkes, S (2000) Using ICT in primary mathematics. London: David Fulton.

Freudenthal, H (1968) 'Why to teach mathematics so as to be useful'. Educational Studies in Mathematics 1: 3-8.

Freudenthal, H (1991) Revisiting mathematics education. China lectures. Dordrecht: Kluwer Academic Publishers.

Fuson, K C, et al. (1982) 'The acquisition of and elaboration of the number word sequence' in Brainerd, C J (ed) Progress in cognitive development: children's logical and mathematical cognition. New York: Springer-Verlag.

Gates, P (2001) 'What is an/at issue in mathematical education', in Gates, P (ed) Issues in mathematics teaching. London: Routledge.

Gelman, R and Gallistel, CR (1986) The child's understanding of number. Cambridge, MA: Harvard University Press.

Gravemeijer, K (1997) 'Mediating between concrete and abstract', in Nunes, T and Bryant, P (eds) *Learning and teaching mathematics: an international perspective.* Hove: Psychology Press.

Gravemeijer, K (2001) 'Fostering a dialectic relation between theory and practice', in Anghileri, J (ed) *Principles and practices in arithmetic teaching.* Buckingham: Open University Press.

Greer, B (1993) 'The mathematical modelling perspective on wor(l)d problems'. *Journal of Mathematical Behaviour,* 12: 239-50.

Harries, T and Sutherland, R (1997) 'Primary school mathematics textbooks: An international comparison', in Thompson, I (ed) *Issues in teaching numeracy in primary schools.* Buckingham: Open University Press.

Haylock, D and Cockburn, A (1989) *Understanding early years mathematics.* London: Paul Chapman.

Hopkins, C, Gifford, S and Pepperell, S (1996) *Mathematics in the primary school: A sense of progression.* London: David Fulton.

Houssart, J and Evans, H (2003) 'Approaching algebra through sequence problems: Exploring children's strategies'. *Research in Mathematics Education,* 5:197-214.

Hughes, M (1986) *Children and number: difficulties in learning mathematics.* Oxford: Blackwell.

Hughes, M (1986) 'Bridge that gap'. *Child Education,* 63:13-15.

Hughes, M, Desforges, C and Mitchell, C (2000) *Numeracy and beyond: Applying mathematics in the primary school.* Buckingham: Open University Press.

Jeffcoat, M, Jones, M, Mansergh, J, Mason, J, Sewell, H and Watson, A (2004) *Primary questions and prompts.* Derby: Association of Teachers of Mathematics.

Jones, L (1994) *Mathematics teaching.* Association of Teachers of Mathematics.

Jones, L (1994) 'Reasoning, logic and proof at Key Stage 2'. *Mathematics in School,* November: 6-8.

Jones, L (2003) 'The problem with problem solving', in Thompson, I (ed) *Enhancing primary mathematics teaching.* Buckingham: Open University Press.

Kelly, P 'Children's experiences of mathematics' in *Conference Proceedings of British Society for Research in Learning Mathematics,* vol. 23, no. 2.

Knight, P, Pennant, J and Piggott, J (2004) 'What does it mean to "Use the interactive whiteboard" in the daily mathematics lesson?', in *Micromath,* Summer.

Mason, J, Graham, A, Pimm, D and Gowar, N (1985) *Routes to/roots of algebra.* Milton Keynes: Open University Press.

McGuinness, C (1999) *From thinking skills to thinking classrooms.* www.dfes.gov.uk/research/data/uploadfiles/RB115.doc

McGuinness, C, Sheehy, N, Curry, C and Eakin, A (2003) 'Teaching thinking through infusion: ACTS in Northern Ireland.' Navcon2k3. Adelaide: University of Flinders; available at www.sustainablethinkingclassrooms.qub.ac.uk/Navcon_Keynote.ppt

Mercer, N (2000) *Words and minds.* London: Routledge.

Mercer, N and Wegerif, R (1998) 'Is "exploratory talk" productive talk?', in Littleton, K and Light, P (eds) *Learning with computers: Analysing productive interactions.* London: Routledge.

Merttens, R (1997) 'Family numeracy', in Thompson, I (ed) *Issues in teaching numeracy in primary school.* Buckingham: Open University Press.

Monaghan, F, 'Thinking better – Using ICT to develop collaborative thinking and talk in mathematics', *British Society for Research in Learning Mathematics* (24, 2), School of Education, University of Birmingham.

Montague-Smith, A, (1997) *Mathematics in Nursery Education.* London: David Fulton.

Munn, P (1997) 'Children's beliefs about counting', in Thompson, I (ed) *Teaching and learning early number*. Buckingham: Open University Press.

Murphy, C (2003) 'A theoretical comparison of the teaching of mental calculation strategies in England and the Netherlands'. *Research in Mathematics Education*, 5:123-37.

Murray, J (2000) 'Mental mathematics', in Koshy, V, Ernest, P and Casey, R (eds) *Mathematics for primary teachers*. London: Routledge.

Nickson, M (2000) *Teaching and learning mathematics: A teacher's guide to recent research*. London: Continuum.

Nunes, T, Schliemann, A and Carraher, D (1993) *Street mathematics and school mathematics*. Cambridge: Cambridge University Press.

Nunes, T and Bryant, P (1996) *Children doing mathematics*. Oxford: Blackwell.

OFSTED (2002) *ICT in Schools*. London: OFSTED.

OFSTED www.ofsted.gov.uk / reports / (information on inspections of provision).

Papert, S (1980) *Mindstorms: Children, computers and powerful ideas*. Brighton: Harvester Press.

Passey, D et al (2004) *The motivational effect of ICT on pupils*. DfES.

Perks, P, 'The interactive whiteboard: Implications for software and design', *British Society for Research in Learning Mathematics*, (22, 1). School of Education, University of Birmingham.

Poulter, T and Basford, J (2003) *Using ICT in Foundation Stage teaching*. Exeter: Learning Matters.

Pratt, N (2002) *Mathematics as thinking*. Mathematics Teaching, 181: 34-7.

QCA (2000) *Guidance on meeting the requirements of gifted and talented pupils*. Suffolk: QCA Enterprises.

QCA/DfEE (2000) Curriculum guidance for the Foundation Stage. London: QCA.

Riley, M S, Greeno, J G and Heller, J I (1983) 'Development of children's problem-solving ability in arithmetic', in Ginsburg, H (ed) *The development of mathematical thinking*. New York: Academic Press.

Rowe, M B (1974) 'Wait time and rewards as instructional variables, their influence on language, logic and fate control'. *Journal of Research in Science Teaching*, 11: 81-94.

Ruthven, K (1999) 'The pedagogy of calculator use', in Thompson, I (ed) *Issues in teaching numeracy in primary schools*. Buckingham: Open University Press, pp195-206.

Sharp, J, Potter, J, Allen, J and Loveless, A (2000) *Achieving QTS Primary ICT: Knowledge, understanding and practice*. Exeter: Learning Matters.

Siraj-Blatchford, I, Sylva, K, Muttock, S, Gilden, R and Bell, D (2002) *Researching effective pedagogy in the early years: Research report No. 356*. Institute of Education, University of London and Department of Educational Studies, University of Oxford.

Skemp, R (1976) 'Relational understanding and instrumental understanding'. *Mathematics Teaching*, 77: 20-6.

Skemp, R (1987) *The psychology of learning mathematics*. London: Lawrence Erlbaum.

Skemp, R (1989) *Mathematics in the primary school*. London: Routledge.

Smith, H (1999) *Opportunities for information communication technology in the primary school*. Stoke on Trent: Trentham Books.

Streefland, L (1985) *Wiskunde als activiteit en de realiteit als bron* ('Mathematics as an activity and reality as source'), NieuweWiskrant, 5(1): 60-7.

Streefland, L (1991) *Fractions in realistic mathematics education: A paradigm of developmental research*. Dordrecht: Kluwer Academic Publishers.

Sylva, K, Melhuish, E, Simmons, P, Siraj-Blatchford, I, Taggart, B and Elliott, K (2003) *The effective provision of pre-school education (EPPE) project: Findings from the pre-school period*. Institute of Education, University of London. DfES.

Tall, D (2002b) *A tribute to Richard Skemp*, at www.warwick.ac.uk/staff/David.Tall/ downloads.html

Teubal, E and Nesher, P (1991) 'Order of mention vs order of events as determining factors in additive word problems: A developmental approach', in Durkin, K and Shire, B (eds) *Language in mathematical education: Research and practice*. Milton Keynes: Open University Press.

Thompson, I (1997) 'Mental and written algorithms: Can the gap be bridged?', in *Teaching and learning early number*. Buckingham: Open University Press..

Thompson, I (2003) 'Deconstructing the National Numeracy Strategy's approach to calculation', in *Enhancing primary mathematics teaching*. Buckingham: Open University Press.

Thompson, I (2004) *Issues in Teaching Numeracy in Primary Schools*. Buckingham: Open University Press.

Thompson, I (2004) *Enhancing Primary Mathematics Teaching*. Buckingham: Open University Press.

Thompson, I and Bramald, R (2002) *An investigation of the relationship between young children's understanding of the concept of place value and their competence at mental addition*. University of Newcastle.

Thompson, I and Smith, F (1999) *Mental calculation strategies for the addition and subtraction of 2-digit numbers (Report for the Nuffield Foundation)*. Newcastle upon Tyne: University of Newcastle upon Tyne.

Treffers, A (1978) *Wiskobas doelgericht* ('Wiskobas goal-directed'). Utrecht: IOWO.

Treffers, A (1987) *Three dimensions. A model of goal and theory description in mathematics instruction – the Wiskobas project*. Dordrecht: Reidel Publishing Company.

Treffers, A (1991) 'Didactical background of a mathematics program for primary education', in Streefland, L *Realistic mathematics education in primary schools*. Utrecht: Utrecht University.

Treffers, A and Beishuizen, M (1999) 'Realistic mathematics education in the Netherlands', in Thompson, I (ed) *Issues in teaching numeracy*. Buckingham: Open University Press.

TTA (2002) *Qualifying to teach: Handbook of guidance*. London: TTA.

University of London and Department of Educational Studies, University of Oxford.

van den Heuvel-Panhuizen, M (1999) 'Context problems and assessment: Ideas from the Netherlands', in Thompson, I (ed) *Issues in teaching numeracy*. Buckingham: Open University Press.

van den Heuvel-Panhuizen, M (2000) *Mathematics education in the Netherlands: A guided tour*. Freudenthal Institute CD-ROM for ICME-9. Utrecht: Utrecht University (available at www.fi.uu.nl/en/rme/TOURdef+ref.pdf).

van den Heuvel-Panhuizen, M (2001) 'Realistic mathematics education in the Netherlands', in Anghileri, J (ed) *Principles and practices in arithmetic teaching*. Buckingham: Open University Press.

van den Heuvel-Panhuizen, M (2002) 'Realistic mathematics education as work in progress', in F L Lin (ed) *Common sense in mathematics education, Proceedings of 2001. The Netherlands and Taiwan Conference on Mathematics Education*. Taipei, Taiwan: National Taiwan Normal University.

Verschaffel, L and De Corte, E (1997) 'Word problems: A vehicle for promoting authentic mathematical understanding and problem solving in the primary school?', in Nunes, T and Bryant, P *Learning and teaching mathematics: An international perspective*. Hove: Psychology Press.

Verschaffel, L, Greer, B and De Corte, E (2000) *Making sense of word problems*. Lisse: Swets and Zeitlinger.

Verschaffel, L, De Corte, E and Lasure, S (1994) 'Realistic considerations in mathematical modelling of school arithmetic word problems'. *Learning and Instruction*, 4: 273-94.

Visser, J (2002) 'Mathematics, inclusion and pupils,' *Mathematics Teaching* no. 179.

Wegerif, R and Dawes, L (2004) *Thinking and Learning with ICT; raising achievement in primary classrooms*. London: Routledge.

Wood (1987) *Measurement and assessment in education and psychology*. London: Falmer Press.

Worthington, M and Caruthers, E (2003) *Children's mathematics: Making marks, making meaning*. London: Paul Chapman.

Index

Algebraic thinking 20-5
  activity 21-2
  comparison of strategies 23-4
  drawing approach 22-5
  evidence of children's pre-algebraic
    thinking 22-6
  generalisations 21
  investigation 22
  patterns, use of 22
  'relationship' approach 23
  sequence of patterns made from squares
    and circles 23-4
  table of results 24-5

Catering for range of mathematical abilities
  95-104
  exclusion 95-7
  gifted children 101-3
  inclusion 99-101
    differentiation, and 100-1
    disability, and 100
    numeracy hour 100
    sharing learning experience 100-1
  inclusion and the able child 101-4
  lack of confidence of teacher, and 95-6
  mathematics experiences outside school
    96
  special educational needs, 95-8. see also
    Special educational needs
  talented children 101-4
Computers. see ICT
Contexts for children's mathematical
  learning 47-56
  assessment questions 51-4
  children's interpretation of 54-6
  difficulty of moving from concrete to
    abstract 48
  exploration of mathematical vocabulary
    49-50
  language of maths 47-50
  learning at home 49-50
  'realistic' responses 55-6
  reflecting on use of contexts in classroom
    52-3
  relationship with real life 56
  textbooks 51-2

translations 49

Effective teaching of mathematics 87-94
  assessment for learning 88-91
  balance between adult-directed and
    child-initiated play 91
  choice of tasks 88
  concentration, and 91
  dialogue 88-9
  discussions 88-9
  evolution of effective teaching 88-90
  homework exercises 89-90
  individual learning 92-3
  learning, and 87
  pedagogy 91-4
  play, and 91-2
  quality of feedback 89-90
  questions by teacher 89-90
  self-initiated play 93
  shopping experience 93
  small group learning 92-3
  style 87
  tests 89-90

ICT 75-8
  analysis of range of software 81
  behaviour, impact on 84
  communication principle 80-2
  deliberate decision to use 80-1
  development of children's learning 80-1
  enhanced resources 83-4
  factors influencing decisions about using
    76
  fascination, and 84
  'fun', and 82
  interactive electronic whiteboard 78-9
  internalisation, and 83
  investigation of patterns 84-5
  large enough to see 77-8
  learning environments 83-4
  Luddites 79
  making decision about 75-6, 83-4
  meaning 75-8
  motivational impact on learning 82-3
  nature of computers 80-1
  organisational strategy 80-1

pedagogical 76-9
perceived obligations 76
positive motivation 83
PowerPoint 79
practical considerations 80
'pupil talk' 80
raised expectations, and 83
research 79
securing engagement 82-4
specific groups of pupils, impact on 84
students and the computer 80-1
teacher, role of 81
teaching environments 83-4
three-part IRF interaction 80
use of 76-80
utilitarian 76-9
Instrumental understanding 7-11
Interactive electronic whiteboard 78-9
contexts in which utilised 79
interactivity 79
saving 78
writing 78

Language of mathematics 47-8
'makes' 50
need to learn and understand 48
'table' 50
'take away' 50
Learning to count 29-36
abstraction principle 31
cardinal principle 30-1
counting principles prone to difficulty
and error 32
developing counting skills in the nursery
29-31
difficulty of 29
nursery rhymes 32
order-irrelevance principle 31
place value 33-6
column value 34-5
'face value' 34
importance of 33
mental calculation strategies 36
quantity value 34-5
stage model 35
understanding of 33-5
principles involved 29-33
rote-learning 32
songs 32
stable-order principle 30

McGuinness Report 17-18

Making decision about mathematics and
ICT, 82-93. see also ICT
Mathematical understanding, nature of 7-16
Brown, M on 8-9
children's experiences of mathematics
13-14
conception 1: labourer 13
conception 2: mechanic 13-14
conception 3: performer 14
conception 4: craftsperson 14
conception 5: academic 14
'grounded theory' 15-16
instrumental understanding 10-12
National Numeracy Strategy 9
perspectives 7
political influence, and 11-16
relational understanding 10-12
'requirements of the state' 9
Skemp, R on 10-12
social and cultural influences 16
swings of the pendulum 7-8
Mental and written calculation strategies 37-
45
'bugs' 41
chunking method 43-4
debate between 38-43
engaging in mathematics as human
activity 41
high profile of mental calculation 41
informal procedure 44
mental algorithms, nature of 39-40
methods of teaching calculations 38
standard written algorithms, nature of
38-9
standard written methods 42-3
strategies used by children to solve
division problems 43-4
high level chunking 43-4
low level chunking 44
standard algorithm for division 44
written methods, resort to 41

National Numeracy Strategy 9

PowerPoint 79
Problem-solving 59-74
categorising using and applying tasks 60
Cockroft Report 59
development of reasoning skills 63-4
everyday contexts 73
exploratory 61-5
flexibility of approach 64

horizontal mathematising 65-6
importance of 59
intervention by teacher 63-4
'investigation', and 59-60
meaning 59
purpose of teaching 73
realistic mathematics education, 60,
    69-73
see also Realistic mathematics education
    reasoning, logic and proof at Key
    Stage 2, 61-2
traditional treatment in UK 60
vertical mathematising 66-7
word problems 64-9
    categorisation 68
    complexities of solving 67-8
    solving 68
    uncoupling mathematics from context
        of problem 68

Realistic mathematics education 69-73
basis of 69-70
bus problem 70-2
connected models as backbone of
    progress 72-3
'daily life' experiences 72
example 69-70
focus of 69-70
functioning of 72-3

Relational understanding 10-12

Special educational needs 97-8
    inclusion 98
    mathematics, and 97-8
    mathematics as rigidly hierarchical
        subject, and 98-9
    meaning 98
Standard written algorithms
    nature of 38-9

Teaching children to think mathematically
    17-28
    algebraic thinking 20-5
    core concepts in framework for
        developing thinking skills 17-20
    forms of interaction 26
    framework for analysing talk in
        classroom 27
    'high-level thinking' 19
    McGuiness Report 17-18
    nature of mathematical thinking 20
    personal response 28
    Pratt, N on 25-7
    suitable tasks 19
    teachers as models of thinkers 19
    teaching strategies, and 25-8
    'thought control', forms of 26-7